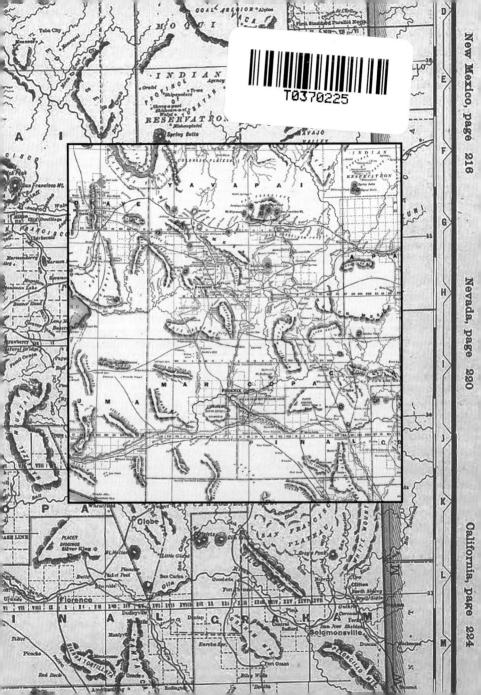

RAILROAD AND COUNTY
MAP OF
ARIZONA.
Geo. F. Cram, Engraver and Publisher, Chicago.

EXPLANATION
Railroads ——————
STATE CAPITOL ✪   County Seat ⊙   Money Order P.O. ⊙

WELLS FARGO & CO
OPERATE ALL ROADS.

ARIZONA
COCKTAILS

AN ELEGANT COLLECTION OF
OVER 100 RECIPES INSPIRED BY
THE GRAND CANYON STATE

ASONTA BENETTI

CIDER MILL
PRESS

BOOK
PUBLISHERS

ARIZONA COCKTAILS

ISBN-13: 978-1-40034-901-2
ISBN-10: 1-40034-901-X

This book may be ordered by mail from the publisher. Please include $5.99 for postage and handling. Please support your local bookseller first!

Books published by Cider Mill Press Book Publishers are available at special discounts for bulk purchases in the United States by corporations, institutions, and other organizations. For more information, please contact the publisher.

Cider Mill Press Book Publishers
"Where good books are ready for press"
501 Nelson Place
Nashville, Tennessee 37214
cidermillpress.com

Typography: Kiln Serif Regular, Copperplate, Sackers, Warnock

Photography credits on page 272

Printed in India

24 25 26 27 28 REP 5 4 3 2 1

First Edition

CONTENTS

INTRODUCTION

BUT FIRST: A HISTORY LESSON

Fondly referred to by locals as State 48, Arizona has been inhabited by various groups of people for thousands of years, all of whom have left their influence and mark on the AZ of today.

From the canal system built by the Hohokam that's still in use today to the cliff dwellings of ancestral Puebloans in Northern Arizona, remnants of prehistoric cultures are everywhere you look. These civilizations inhabited the area for thousands of years before mysteriously disappearing around the fifteenth century. Soon they were replaced by the Spanish, who were looking for gold but found the Grand Canyon instead. Eventually, in the mid-1500s, Francisco Vázquez de Coronado claimed the vast swath of today's southwestern United States for Spain; historical missions like San Xavier del Bac in southern Arizona were established during the centuries that followed.

Cliff dwellings, Canyon de Chelley

Casa Grande Ruins National
Park near Coolidge

San Xavier del Bac, near Tucson, circa 1870

Phoenix in 1908

By 1853, all of Arizona was included as part of the New Mexico territory after treaties and purchases with Mexico to define the southern border. While the official Mexican period of Arizona's history lasted only a few decades, the impact of Mexican heritage and culture is infinitely deep.

On February 14, 1912, Arizona achieved statehood. Today, Phoenix is the fifth most populous city in the country after Arizona saw significant population growth in the twenty-first century. And why wouldn't you want to flock to the Grand Canyon State? The southern region is home to a huge section of the Sonoran Desert, the only place where the saguaro cacti grow amid beautiful desert flora.

Northern Arizona is dotted with pine trees, national parks, and red rocks. There are three American Viticultural Areas across the state, the first International Dark Sky Community (Flagstaff), and a UNESCO City of Gastronomy (Tucson). The population is as diverse as the climate; immigration from across Latin America has created a melting pot of cultures. The Navajo Nation is the largest tribal group in the country, and Arizona's Native population extends to numerous other Indigenous communities. Then there's the impact of residents from India, Southeast Asia, Africa, and elsewhere.

I know you're here for cocktails, but this is important, I promise.

Arizona—Phoenix in particular—has a reputation as a place of transience. Deservedly so, as its population growth—it was the fastest-growing big city in America in the 2010s—was historically driven by people moving for the better weather and lower cost of living. Few of my classmates in the mid-2000s were actually from Arizona, and neither was I. However, things are slowly changing, and younger generations are being born here, growing up here, and living in neighborhoods that now have defined identities. At the same time, there has been a significant rise in Arizona's culinary and nightlife profile, which means residents see their own backyard as a destination for summer staycations, weekend partying, and noteworthy nights out. We have chefs that are winning James Beard awards. We have bars winning top-four nominations for the 2024 Tales of the Cocktail Foundation Spirited Awards and being placed among North America's 50 Best Bars. We have reasons to be here now—reasons beyond our Old West past and the Whiskey Row saloons of Prescott, which are wonderful and a great part of our tapestry, but places that are celebrating how to eat and drink today.

In this exciting time, it's important to remember that the pieces that have shaped Arizona started long before the residential boom of the last few decades. Arizona has a unique identity, and to see facets of that come through in cocktail ingredients, bar inspirations, and drinks sitting in front of customers against one of those show-stopping sunsets has been a joy for this almost-native Arizonan.

ARIZONA'S COCKTAIL HISTORY

While the history of Arizona spans thousands of years, when it comes to cocktails, the timeline is a little briefer. The list of original Arizona cocktails is, frankly, not extensive. However, we do have a couple up our sleeves—one of which may come as a surprise.

One of the first cocktails ever created in the Southwest—the Arizona Statehood—was the work of bartender Mike O'Leary in 1910, two years before the state was even officially in the Union. However, in June 1910, Congress passed the statehood bill for Arizona that provided the final pathway to becoming the forty-eighth state. In celebration, O'Leary created this mixed drink at the Ford Hotel in Phoenix, where city hall currently sits today.

In 1915, five years after O'Leary presented the Arizona Statehood to the world, Arizona became a dry state, and the drink largely passed to the annals of history. Luckily, local watering hole legend Joshua James of Born & Raised Hospitality resurrected it, presenting an updated version in 2018, which you can find on page 14.

The Ford Hotel

The Arizona Biltmore

While the Arizona Statehood did not leave as prominent a mark on the world cocktail stage, the next homegrown drink did. The Tequila Sunrise (see the recipe on page 160) originated at the historic Arizona Biltmore, a resort in the heart of Phoenix known for its Frank Lloyd Wright architecture and Golden Age glamour.

Invented in the 1930s, the Tequila Sunrise is credited to the Arizona Biltmore's longtime bartender, Gene Sulit. As legend recalls, a guest asked Sulit to make him a refreshing drink to take poolside—and to surprise him with its flavor. Sulit rose to the challenge, and the result was a delicious blend of soda and tequila with crème de cassis and fresh lime juice. Because of the density of crème de cassis, it settled at the bottom of the glass, creating the gradient of colors that mimics a sunrise—hence the name. It's somewhat befitting that the best-known cocktail to come out of Arizona also honors our famous sunrises.

ARIZONA STATEHOOD

In 2018, Joshua James of Born & Raised Hospitality revived this century-old recipe. "The original recipe is very simple. It is as follows: A dash of gum. A dash of angostura. A half jigger of rye. A half jigger of dubonnet. Fill with ginger ale and sink a cherry in it," says James. "Mine is a modern adaptation, embodying the blending of whiskey and ginger alongside sweeter ingredients to make a palatable cocktail that was popular at hotels during that era." Although James no longer serves his version at his establishments, his updated recipe allows for anyone to toast Arizona at home.

GLASSWARE: Collins glass
GARNISH: Dehydrated orange slice, brandy-soaked cherry

- 1 oz. | 30 ml Rittenhouse Straight Rye Whisky
- ½ oz. | 15 ml Lillet Rouge
- ½ oz. | 15 ml Iconic Cocktail Co. Ginga Syrup
- ¼ oz. | 7.5 ml Small Hand Foods Gum Syrup
- 2 dashes Angostura bitters
- Canada Dry Tonic Water, to top

1. Combine all of the ingredients, except for the tonic water, in a collins glass with ice and stir.
2. Top with tonic water and garnish with a dehydrated orange slice and a brandy-soaked cherry.

ARIZONA'S COCKTAIL
SCENE TODAY

One thing Arizona has never lacked is sports and cultural events. Growing up here as a creative type, I was never bored.

But while the events and museums were great, downtown Phoenix was sorely lacking in nightlife options. It was simply a place people drove to during the week for work and for the above activities on the weekend. There was no reason to hang out, no great places for pre-curtain drinks or post-concert cocktails.

A few people were trying to make something happen. MercBar, which opened in 1996 near the Biltmore area, was really a Phoenix pioneer when it came to cocktail lounges. It was sleek and sexy—rare for the town at that time. But even it was modeled after a venue in New York, showing that Phoenix was a city that had yet to express itself. Today, it's all different.

You can walk from a Suns game to Bitter & Twisted Cocktail Parlour in the heart of the city, right down the street from Little Rituals, both of which have won numerous national and international awards. You might plan to grab a drink at Quartz Bar before watching a show at the Van Buren. Arizona Cocktail Weekend—now a must-do event in the spring—continues to expand every year, showcasing dozens of bars, bartenders, and drinks for an exponentially growing audience. We've changed; now the highlight of the night isn't just the event but the reservation you scored for afterward.

Trailblazers like Ross Simon helped light the torch; others, like Joshua James and Adrian Galindo, have continued to add gasoline to the fire. The glow coming off of Arizona's cocktail scene is impossible to ignore. Simon and I spoke about hiring the right team for a cocktail bar and his passion for teaching people how to bartend as a profession and a skill set. "I'm a big fan of taking on people who are positive, enthusiastic, with can-do attitudes because it's the one thing I can't teach," he said. And he's right. Among the spotlights and recipe intros, I've tried to capture not just the most influential voices in Arizona's cocktail scene but also the dedicated bartenders and mixologists who you might not know (yet). They are the heart of this flourishing industry and we're proud of all of them.

HOW TO DRINK LIKE A LOCAL

ATTEND THE WASTE MANAGEMENT PHOENIX OPEN
Virtually everyone in Phoenix goes to the Open at least once, and a vast percentage of them could not tell you anything about the golf competition going on. It's a chance to socialize, enjoy being outdoors in February, and drink nonstop.

LINGERING MAY NOT BE IN THE CARDS

The idea of whiling away an entire evening over sophisticated drinks in dim light is lovely. Unfortunately, Phoenix is a big city, and a lot of people probably want your seat at the bar. A significant number of cocktail bars in the Valley are in smaller locations or simply in high demand, so you should be prepared for a time limit, most likely ninety minutes.

PLAN AHEAD

The reservations game is a strong one in the Phoenix metro area; almost all cocktail bars take them, and some require them. For the ones that don't have a reservation system, take heed and be prepared to wait hours on a Friday or Saturday night.

TACOS ARE ALWAYS A GOOD IDEA

Neither Arizona nor Phoenix is known for operating 24/7. In fact, except for a few specific locales, visitors may be shocked at how early establishments wrap things up for the night; a closing time of 9 or 10 p.m. is not unusual. If you get the post-drinks, late-night munchies, a twenty-four-hour takeout Mexican place is the way to go. Look for a mom-and-pop place, a Filiberto's, or one of the many -berto iterations around the state.

CHECK OUT YOUR HOTEL BAR

Arizona is a vacation destination, so resorts and hotels are plentiful. A well-executed hotel bar offering is crucial. A recent push has seen these properties revamp their bars into destinations in their own right, sometimes partnering with outside bar ownership rather than keeping it in-house. It's a great incentive for guests and for locals, who often snag summer staycation deals while riding out the excessive temperatures.

GET OUT ON THAT PATIO

For six to seven months a year, Arizonans love to brag about the weather, which includes sipping cocktails while watching sunsets as the rest of the country de-ices their windshields. When the weather is good, check out the patios at local bars, which can have some of the best views across the cities.

KEEP THE WATER COMING

It's hot. That's a given. So make sure to hydrate while you're drinking. Enough said?

YES, TEQUILA IS GOOD BUT...

In the desert, Margaritas are obviously a must. But it's worth expanding beyond your favorite tequila-based drink for spirits that are crafted in Arizona—and there are a lot of them. From whiskey to sake, Arizona has a strong homegrown spirits presence, so make sure to embrace them when you can. And if you want to switch it up, check out Arizona's breweries and wineries, which are numerous and award winning.

IT'S AN EVER-CHANGING WORLD

As discussed, the words "Arizona" and "cocktail culture" were incompatible until relatively recently. Since then, the cocktail presence here in State 48 has exploded into one that residents are extremely proud of—but we're not done yet! New bars, concepts, and drinks are constantly cropping up, so don't be afraid to see what's new out there.

WHAT YOU NEED FOR AN ARIZONA BAR

Not every recipe in this book is something you could easily pull together after work on a Tuesday night. Some might require specialty implements or are served in a unique way (flaming skull glass, anyone?), but the majority can be created with the glasses and tools given below.

The most important thing to remember is to keep it flexible for both indoor and outdoor living. You want cocktails you can mix in the kitchen and serve on the patio under the misters. Consider a smaller portable bar that can come outdoors or stay out there when the weather is good so you're not trying to enjoy a pool day and then running to the house for more drinks. And it may not be totally couth, but get some nonbreakable stemware as well. Your cocktail may be a work of art, but elegant glasses plus floating in pools doesn't equal a good idea.

GLASSWARE

The type of glass really does matter; the vessel impacts how a bartender builds a drink, how it releases flavors, how it smells, and how heat from a hand transfers to the cocktail. Keep a collection of highball/collins glasses, lowball/rocks glasses, coupes, Nick & Noras, and martini glasses in your bar cabinet. Those five versatile types will carry you through almost all of the recipes in this book.

TOOLS

Make sure to have the basics on hand; a lot of cocktail magic can be made with just a few critical instruments.

- Yarai/heavy mixing glass
- Barspoon
- Shaker tins
- Strainers, both Hawthorne and fine-mesh
- Jigger
- Handheld/manual juicer
- Fruit peeler
- Stick/immersion blender
- Smoker/smoking setup
- Kitchen torch
- Kitchen scale

ESSENTIALS

20% SALINE SOLUTION: Combine 80 grams (80 ml) water with 20 grams salt (kosher, sea salt—your choice) and stir until the salt is dissolved. Keep the solution in a dropper bottle. For a 10% solution, use 10 grams salt.

SIMPLE SYRUP: In a small saucepan over medium-low heat, combine 1 cup water and 1 cup sugar and simmer, stirring until the sugar is dissolved. Remove the syrup from heat and allow it to cool. To make 2:1 (thick) simple syrup, double the sugar. To make demerara simple syrup, use demerara sugar. To make flavored simple syrup (cinnamon, mint, or ginger, for example), add the fresh ingredients during either the simmering or the steeping phase and strain before use.

HONEY SYRUP: In a small saucepan, combine 1 cup almost-boiling water with 1 cup honey and stir until the honey is dissolved. Then allow the syrup to cool.

STRAIN: Use a Hawthorne strainer to prevent the ice from your cocktail shaker tin or mixing glass from going with your cocktail into your glassware. To double-strain, do the same thing but also place a conical fine-mesh strainer over the glassware, preventing citrus, herbal, or other small solids from going into the glass.

SUPPLIES

To really lean into an AZ-style setup, consider stocking the following items as part of your everyday bar.

AGAVE-BASED SPIRITS: Invest in a really good blanco tequila so you can always whip up a classic Margarita or one of the many versions in this book. But don't stop there! There are so many wonderful agave-based spirits that extend beyond tequila; keep some different mezcals on hand, plus raicilla and bacanora. Go further into tequila with reposados and añejos to provide a rich depth to drinks.

LOCAL DISTILLATIONS: Look for Arizona brands at your local store or online, such as Whiskey Del Bac, ROXX Vodka, Arizona Sake, and Blue Clover Distillery to support the distillation efforts of those pushing the boundaries of craft distilling in the 48th state.

CITRUS: Don't forget that one of the state's five C's is citrus, which grow in abundance here. Fresh juice from lemons, limes, and grapefruits are key to building a significant number of cocktails within these pages, so get the actual fruit to squeeze whenever possible. Citrus is also crucial as a garnish, so use the peels or dehydrate them as the final flourish.

NORTHERN ARIZONA

SANCHO

THE GAMBLE

SEDONA NEW FASHION

THE DIRTY VERDE

SPIRITED BRÛLEÉ

BOYNTON BLUEBERRY

G-FORCE

PISCO SOUR PRIMITIVO

THE EMPRESS

SEDONA MEDICINA

SUCKER PUNCH

SOLTERA

THE BASTARD SON

There may be some bias toward this section due to my love of Northern Arizona. I have cherished memories of camping at the Mogollon Rim lakes, taking spur-of-the-moment day trips to Sedona with friends, and spending cool summer days in Flagstaff with great food and views.

The author's subjectivity aside, there is good reason to begin this journey at the top of the state. Towns across the area are rapidly growing, not just because of visitors discovering all the hidden gems across the pines and mountains but also due to residents looking to escape the Valley heat. Recent growth has spurred strong development in the food-and-beverage space—yes, you can still go to a saloon for that Old West kick, but you can also get a handcrafted cocktail served alongside creative and award-winning dining. Add some lower temps, leaves changing colors, and snowflakes falling, and you'll see why Northern AZ is the complete package.

MICHAEL HOPPER, ATRIA

What's your favorite cocktail to make?

I enjoy making an Old Fashioned. They're easy to mess up, so when someone comes in and says, "Can you make a good Old Fashioned?" I instantly get excited. That drink alone can tell you a lot about the person making your cocktails.

How did you get interested in cocktails and mixology?

I was in the navy for four years. When I got out, I still had no idea what I wanted to do. Bartending sounded like fun, so I started learning. The first bar I worked at was a country line-dancing bar where I started as a barback. Once I moved to Flagstaff, I bounced around the town gaining experience at each spot until I landed a job at a cocktail bar called Rendezvous. I learned a lot about cocktails there and how to build them. After a few months, I became the bar manager, which taught me more about the bar business. Being offered the job at Atria has been a game changer for my career. Having amazing chefs in the kitchen has taught me so many different ways to incorporate new ingredients into cocktails.

What influences you as a mixologist?

Trying to figure out different and new flavor combinations to work into a cocktail. I like taking things you wouldn't necessarily think of using and turning them into something awesome. I also love changing people's minds when they come in and say something like, "I don't like mezcal," and I am able to serve them something that completely changes their opinion on a spirit.

How do you draw inspiration from your local area when creating new drinks?

Flagstaff is a one-of-a-kind place. One thing I actually really like is the tourism. Yes, it creates massive traffic delays, but it also brings people from all areas of the world into the restaurant. So being able to create an amazing drink for visitors and knowing that they will go back home and tell their friends or family what they drank is pretty inspiring to me.

What do you find unique about Arizona's cocktail culture?

It's close-knit. Everyone seems to know everyone and is really rooting for people to produce great cocktails. Whenever I go down to Phoenix, it seems like everyone is friends with one another and wants them to succeed even though they work at different bars. The goal is just to have cool places to go and forget about life for a minute.

What are some underrated ingredients you love to use and why?

I've recently been diving into amari for my cocktails. They are a great way to introduce a specific flavor to the drink while also incorporating sweetness. That way the cocktail doesn't become overly saturated with sugar but can have the right balance to showcase the other ingredients.

What's an accomplishment or point of pride in your career?

It's only been five years since I started in this industry, and I believe I am running one of the best bar programs in the state. There are some cocktail giants down in Phoenix I would love to go learn under so I can continue to grow in my craft. But at the end of the day, the accomplishment is creating drinks for people to enjoy. I want people to like the drink they are paying their hard-earned money for.

SANCHO

ATRIA
103 NORTH LEROUX STREET, FLAGSTAFF

Mixologist Michael Hopper believes that this drink can represent all of AZ in one glass. "The inspiration behind the drink was to create a riff of a Vieux Carré with an Arizona twist," he says. The mezcal, reposado, and citrus are all nods to influential flavors in Arizona, and the copper hue that comes off the cocktail is a tie-in to the state's mining history. It's a wonderful salute to State 48.

GLASSWARE: Coupe glass
GARNISH: Orange peel

- 1½ oz. | 45 ml espadín mezcal
- 1 oz. | 30 ml Orange-Infused Reposado Tequila (see recipe)
- ¾ oz. | 22.5 ml Vecchio Amaro del Capo
- ¼ oz. | 7.5 ml agave nectar
- 2 dashes orange bitters

1. Chill a coupe glass. Combine all of the ingredients in a mixing glass with ice and stir.
2. Strain the cocktail into the chilled coupe.
3. Garnish with an orange peel.

ORANGE-INFUSED REPOSADO TEQUILA: In a large mason jar, combine 1 orange, dehydrated or fresh and sliced or cut into wedges, and 1 (750 ml) bottle of reposado tequila. Allow the infusion to sit for 2 to 3 days. Strain and rebottle.

THE GAMBLE

RESTAURANT FORTY1
900 WEST STATE ROUTE 89A, SEDONA

I have always been told that one in ten shishito peppers will be spicy," says mixologist Rachelle Connolly. "Each batch of shishito-infused mezcal we make here at Forty1 has a chance of being hot or not. If you're a gambler and willing to test your luck on a hot margarita with fresh watermelon juice, you'll love The Gamble."

╫

GLASSWARE: Rocks glass
GARNISH: Shishito pepper, blistered

- Orange Chili Salt (see recipe), for the rim
- 2 oz. | 60 ml Shishito-Infused Mezcal (see recipe)
- 3 oz. | 90 ml Watermelon Limeade (see recipe)

1. Wet the rim of a rocks glass, then dip the rim into the Orange Chili Salt.

2. Combine the infused mezcal and limeade in a cocktail shaker and shake for 30 seconds.

3. Pour the cocktail into the rimmed rocks glass over fresh ice.

4. Garnish with the blistered shishito pepper.

SHISHITO-INFUSED MEZCAL: Pour a full bottle of Naran Mezcal into a container with 5 blistered shishito peppers and let it infuse for 24 hours in a cool, dark place. Strain and rebottle.

WATERMELON LIMEADE: In a container, combine 8 oz. (240 ml) fresh watermelon juice, 8 oz. (240 ml) fresh lime juice, 2½ oz. (75 ml) organic agave nectar, and 2½ oz. (75 ml) water and stir to combine.

ORANGE CHILI SALT: In a container, combine 1 cup (241 grams) kosher salt, 1 tablespoon (7½ grams) Mexican chili powder, 1 tablespoon (7½ grams) chorizo seasoning, and the zest of 2 large oranges and mix.

SEDONA NEW FASHION

RESTAURANT FORTY1
900 WEST STATE ROUTE 89A, SEDONA

Summers in Northern Arizona aren't as intense as what Phoenix experiences, and they allow for lots of fresh local fruit. In the Sedona area, it's not uncommon to see trees of sweet apricots, which mixologist Rachelle Connolly transforms into a silky puree. Added to bourbon, it's a great Sedona twist on the classic Old Fashioned.

GLASSWARE: Rocks glass
GARNISH: Dehydrated apricot chip

- **2 oz. | 60 ml Old Forester 100 Proof Bourbon**
- **1¾ oz. | 52 ml Apricot Puree (see recipe)**
- **4 dashes Angostura orange bitters**

1. Combine all of the ingredients in a Yarai mixing glass and stir for 30 seconds.
2. Strain the cocktail into a rocks glass over a large ice cube.
3. Smoke with a cocktail smoker for 2 to 3 minutes and garnish with a dehydrated apricot chip.

APRICOT PUREE: In a saucepan over medium-low heat, combine 4 apricots with the pits removed, chopped; ½ cup sugar; and 16 oz. water and simmer for 20 minutes (don't allow the mixture to boil). Remove from heat and let the mixture cool. Once cooled, put the mixture into a blender and blend on high until smooth, 2 to 3 minutes. Strain the puree through a fine-mesh strainer.

THE DIRTY VERDE

RESTAURANT FORTY1
900 WEST STATE ROUTE 89A, SEDONA

I grew up in Cornville, which is nestled in the heart of the Verde Valley," says Rachelle Connolly, the mixologist for Forty1. "The Verde River is one of my favorite rivers here. Locals in the area have always had a nickname for our beloved river: 'The Dirty Verde.' I wanted to make a cocktail that would have both a bright green color, as the Verde River does in the spring, and a spicy kick, like summers in Arizona."

GLASSWARE: Rocks glass

GARNISH: Dehydrated orange slice, flower petals

- Orange Chili Salt (see recipe on page 31)
- 2 oz. | 60 ml Pepper-Infused Tequila (see recipe)
- 1 oz. | 30 ml Luxardo Maraschino Liqueur
- 1 oz. | 30 ml Monin Organic Agave
- 1 oz. | 30 ml fresh lime juice
- Half of an avocado

1. Wet the rim of a rocks glass then dip the rim into the Orange Chili Salt to give the glass a rim.

2. Combine the remaining ingredients in a cocktail shaker with ice and shake vigorously for 60 seconds, until the avocado is incorporated into the mixture.

3. Add fresh ice to the rimmed rocks glass and double-strain the cocktail into the glass.

4. Garnish with a dehydrated orange slice and flower petals.

PEPPER-INFUSED TEQUILA: In a container, combine 1 (750 ml) bottle of Corazón Blanco Tequila, 2 large jalapeño peppers cut in half with seeds removed; 1 poblano pepper, cut into quarters with seeds removed; and 1 red bell pepper, cut into quarters with seeds removed. Let the tequila infusion sit for at least 24 hours before using.

SPIRITED BRÛLÉE

RESTAURANT FORTY1
900 WEST STATE ROUTE 89A, SEDONA

One of the highlights at Forty1 is their Asian-Latin fusion menu that was the brainchild of executive chef David Duncan and mixologist Rachelle Connolly. This particular cocktail speaks more to the Asian influence, inspired by Connolly's favorite anime film; the drink finishes floral and fruity but not too sweet.

||||

GLASSWARE: Rocks glass

GARNISH: Brûleé Chip (see recipe), orange swath

- 2 oz. | 60 ml Roku Gin
- 1 oz. | 30 ml Morello cherry puree
- 1 oz. | 30 ml fresh lemon juice
- 1 oz. | 30 ml Demerara Simple Syrup (see recipe on page 20)
- 3 dashes Bittercube Cherry Bark Vanilla Bitters

1. Combine all of the ingredients in a cocktail shaker with ice and shake it up for 30 seconds.
2. Strain the cocktail into a rocks glass over fresh ice.
3. Garnish with a Brûleé Chip and a ribboned orange swath.

BRÛLEÉ CHIP: Spread sugar on the flesh of half of a zested orange and brûleé it with a kitchen torch until the sugar is golden brown and bubbling. Let it cool.

BOYNTON BLUEBERRY

CHE AH CHI
525 BOYNTON CANYON ROAD, SEDONA

S edona's views are already stunning, but the views from Che Ah Chi at Enchantment Resort are nearly impossible to beat. The property is nestled at the bottom of Boynton Canyon, providing dramatic vistas of Sedona's famous red rock formations. The sweet and refreshing, but also potent, Boynton Blueberry represents Che Ah Chi's salute to the all-important canyon.

GLASSWARE: Coupe glass
GARNISH: Fresh blueberries and lemon wheel on a skewer

- 2 oz. | 60 ml Ypióca Brasilizar Cachaça Prata Classica
- 1 oz. | 30 ml fresh pineapple juice
- ¼ oz. | 7.5 ml blueberry syrup
- 2 dashes lemon bitters

1. Combine all of the ingredients in a cocktail shaker with ice and shake well.
2. Strain the cocktail into a coupe.
3. Garnish with fresh blueberries skewered with a lemon wheel.

G-FORCE

Perhaps the greatest Oaxaca Old Fashioned ever built," says Lisa Dahl, executive chef and owner of the Dahl Restaurant Group. "Elegant tequila meets smoky and mineral-rich mezcal and Aztec chocolate bitters for a sweet and smoky explosion of flavor." It's the perfect complement to dinner at Mariposa, a Latin-inspired grill that sits just off Highway 89A in the heart of Sedona.

GLASSWARE: Rocks glass

GARNISH: Orange zest

- 1½ oz. | 45 ml G4 Reposado Tequila
- ½ oz. | 15 ml Carreño Tepeztate Mezcal
- ¼ oz. | 7.5 ml agave nectar
- 2 dashes Fee Brothers Gin Barrel-Aged Orange Bitters
- 1 dash Fee Brothers Aztec Chocolate Bitters

1. Combine all of the ingredients in a mixing glass.
2. Add a scoop of ice to the glass and stir for approximately 20 seconds.
3. Strain the cocktail over a large ice cube into a rocks glass.
4. Flame an orange zest over the top of the cocktail.
5. Rim and garnish the cocktail glass with the orange zest.

PISCO SOUR PRIMITIVO

MARIPOSA
700 WEST ARIZONA 89A, SEDONA

he Pisco Sour is the original Peruvian craft cocktail, refreshing and easy on the palate. "Invented in the 1920s by bartender Victor Vaughen Morris, the drink has become a part of modern culture in Peru," says Lisa Dahl. "It even has its own national holiday, El Día Nacional del Pisco Sour, on the first Saturday in February. This recipe pays homage to the original creation."

‖

GLASSWARE: Champagne flute
GARNISH: Angostura bitters

- 1½ oz. | 45 ml Caravedo Pisco Mosto Verde Acholado
- ¾ oz. | 22.5 ml fresh lemon juice
- ¾ oz. | 22.5 ml fresh lime juice
- ¾ oz. | 22.5 ml egg white
- 1½ oz. | 45 ml Simple Syrup (see recipe on page 20)

1. Chill a champagne flute. Combine all of the ingredients in a cocktail shaker without ice and dry-shake to froth the egg white.
2. Fill the tin with ice and shake again (wet-shake).
3. Strain the cocktail into the chilled champagne flute
4. Garnish with a dash of bitters.

THE EMPRESS

BUTTERFLY BURGER
6657 AZ-179, SUITE B1, SEDONA

"The Empress has it all—micro-distilled gin mixed with balanced flavors, and it's beautiful in a coupe glass," says venue owner Lisa Dahl. The recipe calls for lavender as an eye-catching garnish; as a low-water plant, lavender grows well in the desert.

⦀

GLASSWARE: Coupe glass
GARNISH: Sprig of rosemary, lemon wedge

- 2 oz. | 60 ml Empress 1908 Indigo Gin
- ¾ oz. | 45 ml Giffard Lavender Syrup
- ¾ oz. | 45 ml fresh lemon juice
- 2 drops 20% Saline Solution (see recipe on page 20)
- 2 oz. | 60 ml prosecco, to top

1. Combine all of the ingredients, except for the prosecco, in a cocktail shaker with ice and shake for about 10 seconds.
2. Strain the cocktail into a coupe and top with the prosecco.
3. Garnish with a fresh or dried sprig of rosemary and a lemon wedge.

SEDONA MEDICINA

DAHL & DILUCA
2321 ARIZONA 89-A, SEDONA

"This cocktail speaks!" says Lisa Dahl. "You will fall in love with the elegant combination of fine tequila and amaro. It's big on alcohol and stunning to view in a chilled martini glass." Dahl & DiLuca has been an Italian dining staple in Sedona for decades, known for its romantic atmosphere and robust menu. You can't go wrong with this Southwestern-Italian twist on a Martini.

⸻ ‖ ⸻

GLASSWARE: Rocks or martini glass
GARNISH: Orange zest

- **1½ oz. | 45 ml Corrido Reposado Tequila**
- **½ oz. | 15 ml Antica Torino Amaro della Sacra**
- **½ oz. | 15 ml Aperol**

1. Combine all of the ingredients in a mixing glass.
2. Add one large scoop of ice and stir at least 20 rotations, or until the cocktail is well chilled.
3. Strain the cocktail into a rocks glass over one large ice cube, or into a well-chilled martini glass.
4. Garnish with an orange zest and present with grace.

BOB KOLAR, THE POINT BAR & LOUNGE

What is your favorite cocktail to make?

I enjoy making cocktails for people that nudge them out of their comfort zone. Preconceived notions or past bad exposure with spirits can really limit a truly exceptional experience. Once you break that barrier and establish trust, you can blow some minds.

How do you draw inspiration from your local area when creating new drinks?

Historically, turning twenty-one in Prescott didn't give you much variety. Every bar was essentially a dive bar with a different coat of paint. My inspiration is simply to bring an elevated cocktail experience to my hometown.

Tell us about some of your favorite ingredients.

Amaro, for sure! I also prefer to make my own bitters as well.

What's one thing about Arizona that you think people don't understand or is misconstrued?

I think it's more an underestimation of what Arizona can offer. People don't really equate Arizona with having a cocktail culture like New York or San Francisco. Once they see all that we have here, they change their tune.

What's an accomplishment or point of pride in your career?

Bringing an elevated cocktail presence to my hometown is my favorite accomplishment. I was told by many people before we opened The Point that a "fancy bar" wasn't needed here in town and that we would fail. Ten years later, we're still going strong, and I am very proud of that.

Anything else you'd like to share?

Phoenix and Tucson have stellar cocktail communities but don't count Northern Arizona out. Flagstaff has several awesome cocktail bars. Cottonwood's Old Town is an up-and-coming food-and-drink destination. Sedona has several world-class resorts with great menus. Since opening the first proper cocktail lounge in Prescott, many other cocktail programs have stepped up their game, with many more businesses opening soon. Come explore ALL of Arizona, it's a beautiful trip!

SUCKER PUNCH

THE POINT BAR & LOUNGE
114 NORTH MONTEZUMA STREET, PRESCOTT

One of the keys to Sucker Punch's success is the muddle technique with the berries and jalapeño. Muddling is a way to lightly mash fruit, spices, or herbs to infuse the liquid of a drink and impact the flavor. To do this, you will need a pestle or muddle stick that can be used to grind ingredients at the bottom of a glass.

GLASSWARE: Rocks glass
GARNISH: Expressed lemon peel

- 4 blueberries
- 2 blackberries
- 1 jalapeño slice
- ¾ oz. | 22.5 ml Agave Nectar Syrup (see recipe)
- ¾ oz. | 22.5 ml fresh lemon juice
- 1½ oz. | 45 ml Mezcal Rayu Espadín Joven
- ¾ oz. | 22.5 ml Alma Tepec Licor de Chile Pasilla Mixe

1. In a cocktail shaker tin, combine the berries, jalapeño, agave nectar, and lemon juice and muddle.
2. Add the mezcal and liqueur to the shaker along with ice and shake.
3. Double-strain the cocktail into a rocks glass with a large cube.
4. Express a lemon peel and add as a garnish.

AGAVE NECTAR SYRUP: In a heatproof container, combine 1 cup agave nectar and 1 cup very hot water and stir until the nectar is dissolved. Allow the syrup to cool.

SOLTERA

Bartender Stephanie Spence recommends an additive-free reposado for this cocktail. "Additive-free" is a movement to be more transparent about what is added to tequilas besides agave, water, and yeast. Certain additional ingredients like coloring, extract, and glycerin are sometimes added to the final mix and the final product is still tequila. However, a growing number of consumers want brands to keep things very simple and eschew these peripherals. Websites like Tequila Matchmaker verify if a brand is truly additive-free and keep an accessible list of products that fit the criteria.

GLASSWARE: Coupe glass
GARNISH: Cucumber ribbon

- ⅛ oz. | 3 ml absinthe, to rinse
- 2 oz. | 60 ml reposado tequila
- ½ oz. | 15 ml Fiorente Elderflower Liqueur
- ½ oz. | 15 ml Dolin Blanc Vermouth
- 3 dashes orange bitters

1. Chill the coupe glass and then rinse with absinthe.
2. Add all the remaining ingredients to a mixing glass with ice and stir.
3. Strain the cocktail into the chilled coupe and garnish with a cucumber ribbon skewered on a bamboo pick.

THE BASTARD SON

THE POINT BAR & LOUNGE
114 NORTH MONTEZUMA STREET, PRESCOTT

Bartender Bobby Joe Kolar uses a rinsing technique with Hamilton Pimento Dram before building the cocktail. Rinsing is a great way to layer in some additional flavor of an ingredient, perhaps a stronger flavor, without adding enough to affect the overall cocktail's balance. To do this, rotate the glass until the interior is coated before pouring out the excess.

GLASSWARE: Rocks glass
GARNISH: Orange peel, expressed; smoke

- ⅛ oz. | 3 ml Hamilton Jamaican Pimento Dram Liqueur, to rinse
- 2 dashes Angostura bitters
- 1½ oz. | 45 ml Rittenhouse Straight Rye Whisky
- ¼ oz. | 7.5 ml Dolin Rouge Vermouth
- ¼ oz. | 7.5 ml Punt e Mes
- ¼ oz. | 7.5 ml Amaro Ramazzotti

1. Rinse the glass with the liqueur and discard the excess.
2. Add one large, clear ice cube to the glass with the bitters.
3. Add the remaining ingredients to the glass and stir.
4. Express the orange peel over the drink then add it as a garnish.
5. Top with a cocktail smoker and give it a little smoke.

TUCSON AND
SOUTHERN ARIZONA

HOLA MUSHASHO

JAGUAR EL JEFE

CAFECITO MARTINI

BAD RAINS

UGLY BUT HONEST

MORE DOLLARS THAN SENSE

FEARLESS VAMPIRE KILLER

SAPIEN LANDING

BIRDIES UP

OBSIDIAN COOL

MANIFEST YOUR NATURE

ucson and Phoenix, Arizona's biggest cities, have had a long-standing, mostly friendly, rivalry, although the intensity increases during the annual Duel in the Desert football game between Arizona State University and University of Arizona. Located two hours south of the capital, Tucson is a cultural mecca for the state and is finally getting some serious recognition for what it has to offer. Just as Northern Arizona is chock-full of artifacts from our ancestral past, there are many points of significance in the south that capture not only Indigenous but Spanish influence.

In 2015, Tucson became the first UNESCO City of Gastronomy in the United States and for good reason. There is strength and support for the city's food heritage, which includes a push to preserve and use native ingredients. Its strong and vibrant cocktail scene is flourishing, spurred on by its diverse and wide-ranging community. Life doesn't seem quite as fast paced down here, and that is a good thing.

HOLA MUSHASHO

This drink tastes like the sun-scorched desert with toasted earthy notes highlighted by the roasted nuttiness of the *chapulín*," says mixologist Kelly Lemons. The chapulín (grasshopper) and beet shrub pays homage to the unique, bold ingredients found in traditional Mexican and Southwestern cuisine.

GLASSWARE: Nick & Nora glass

GARNISH: Tamarind beet fruit leather, chapulín

- 2 oz. | 60 ml Mazot Palmilla
- ¾ oz. | 22.5 ml Amaro Sfumato Rabarbaro
- Dash rhubarb bitters
- ¼ oz. | 7.5 ml Beet & Chapulín Shrub (see recipe)
- Dash Peychaud's bitters

1. Combine all of the ingredients in a mixing glass and stir.
2. Pour the cocktail into a Nick & Nora.
3. Garnish with tamarind beet fruit leather and a chapulín.

BEET & CHAPULÍN SHRUB: In a nonreactive bowl, combine 1 cup apple cider vinegar, 1 cup sugar, ½ cup chapulíns (Mexican dried grasshopper snack), and 1 teaspoon salt and whisk to combine. Add 4 peeled beets, mix, cover, and allow the shrub to macerate for 2 days, stirring occasionally. Fine-strain into a clean jar.

JAGUAR EL JEFE

SONORA MOONSHINE CO.

124 EAST BROADWAY BOULEVARD, TUCSON

Named after El Jefe, an adult male jaguar that was the only wild jaguar verified to live in the United States from 2011 to 2015, primarily seen in the Santa Rita Mountains of Arizona, this drink has a wild side.

GLASSWARE: Coupette glass
GARNISH: Lemon zest, orchid

- 1 oz. | 30 ml Estancia Destilado de Pulque
- ¾ oz. | 22.5 ml Damiana Liqueur
- ½ oz. | 15 ml Granada-Vallet Bitter Pomegranate Liqueur
- ¾ oz. | 22.5 ml Salted Lemon Cordial (see recipe)
- ¾ oz. | 22.5 ml papaya puree
- Dash bitters

1. Combine all of the ingredients in a cocktail shaker with ice and shake.

2. Double-strain the cocktail into a coupette.

3. Garnish with twisted Z-cut lemon zest and an orchid.

SALTED LEMON CORDIAL: First, make Simple Syrup (see recipe on page 20). Then add the zest and juice of 4 lemons, and sea salt flakes, to taste, to the syrup over medium heat. When the mixture reaches a simmer, remove it from heat, whisk until the salt is dissolved, and allow the cordial to cool. Strain.

CAFECITO MARTINI

IGNITE LOUNGE & BAR
15000 NORTH SECRET SPRINGS DRIVE, MARANA

Ignite is nestled in The Ritz-Carlton Dove Mountain property, which sits outside of Tucson in the town of Marana. The area is riddled with archaeological sites that trace the long history of the state, with remnants of life from the Hohokam and Spanish colonists. The desert setting of the property makes it a great place to get away and look at the Tortolita Mountains—with a Cafecito Martini in hand, of course. You can substitute almond milk or coconut milk for the half-and-half.

GLASSWARE: Coupe glass
GARNISH: 3 espresso beans, dusting of cocoa powder

- 1½ oz. | 45 ml Don Julio 1942
- 1 oz. | 30 ml espresso
- ¾ oz. | 22.5 ml Kahlúa
- ¾ oz. | 22.5 ml Baileys Original Irish Cream
- ¾ oz. | 22.5 ml half-and-half
- ¼ oz. | 7.5 ml agave nectar

1. Combine all of the ingredients in a cocktail shaker with ice and shake.
2. Double-strain the cocktail into a coupe.
3. Garnish with 3 espresso beans and a dusting of cocoa powder.

KARL GÓRANOWSKI, TOUGH LUCK CLUB/FENTON FAMILY RESTAURANTS

What's your favorite cocktail to make?

If you made me pick one, it would be a barrel-proof rye 50/50 Manhattan [half whiskey, half vermouth] with an abundance of orange and aromatic bitters.

How did you get interested in cocktails and mixology?

I was mostly interested in drinking, and tending a bar seemed like a great way to make a living and do that. I got a job from a mentor who showed me that cocktail bartending was a real craft. I was blown away, thinking I could have a job where I could be creative and make people happy. I poured myself into learning, and it became not only my passion but also my profession. Now, as a sober bartender, it's broadened my focus to encompass the overall guest experience beyond drinks and service.

Bartending saved my life at a time when I was in a very dark place. Getting sober saved my life from the different dark place bartending had led me to. Get help if you are experiencing issues with mental health or substance abuse. If you aren't here, you can't bring anything to the table. The world needs you more than you think.

What influences you as a mixologist?

My influences come from both inside and outside the service industry. From inside the service industry, I have been influenced by working in a wide range of establishments. From cocktail bars I learned precision and attention to detail, from nightclubs I learned speed and directness, from restaurants I learned service and time management, and from my peers I learned about all the topics outside of cocktails that I needed to know, such as wine and beer.

Outside of the bar world, I have always been influenced by the DIY culture of punk rock, and I have tried to bring that ethos into my work. I take inspiration from a wide range of media and art, including classical literature, professional wrestling, and gaming culture (especially Magic: The Gathering). I have made tribute cocktails to baseball managers, line cooks, labor activists, local legends, fairy-tale frogs, the different biomes in Arizona, and a whole world of other things. I try to look outside the normal and take influences from everything I can.

How do you draw inspiration from your local area when creating new drinks?

Tucson is easy to get inspiration from, as it is a very singular place. We are out here on an island, not surrounded by water but by desert, one hundred miles from the next big city and right on the edge of the United States. That means I bring in a lot from my old pueblo and the area around it whenever I am making a cocktail menu. From cocktails named after our local neighborhoods and geographic landmarks in our area to locally foraged botanicals, I have tried to pay tribute to— but not make a gimmick out of—our own slice of Arizona's landscape. By using an international lens and my experience with cocktailing around the country and the world, I think we have carved out a style that speaks to our town but is relatable to the whole world of cocktails.

What do you find unique about Arizona's cocktail culture?

Arizona's cocktail culture is incredibly varied, and the breadth of amazing places that are all very different from each other is definitely unique from other cities. The differences between bars in Scottsdale, Flagstaff, Tucson, and Phoenix are huge, way bigger than cities in most states. That being said, we have the opportunity to see the whole world, from a hole-in-the-wall to an ultra-lounge, from a sexy cocktail den to a raucous party bar. This incredible range is something that Arizona should embrace and celebrate.

What are some underrated ingredients you love to use and why?

Not underrated by bartenders, but the public sleeps on brandy of all types. I especially like American brandy. Brands like Paul Masson Brandy and Laird's Straight Apple Brandy are working-class regional staples that people love, but the wider world doesn't rate them as the world-class spirits they are.

I also love Heaven Hill products; Mellow Corn is a staple and should be in every bar worth its salt. But the bourbons are really where they hit a home run. The Henry McKenna 10-Year just hits in a way that most ten-year-old American whiskeys don't. The crown jewel for me is the seven-year Heaven Hill Bottled-in-Bond. It's the perfect bourbon as far as age and proof, a real stunner. I know people like it, but this should be the number one most sought-after product out there.

What's one thing about Arizona that you think people don't understand or is misconstrued?

Arizona is massive and has a bit of everything (minus the beach). I don't think people realize how different things are from city to city in the Valley of the Sun, let alone how different Tucson is from Phoenix or how different northern Arizona is from the desert. I think people have this idea that Arizona is all cowboy hats and pickups, when it has that plus so much more. We have everything, every subculture, and our own lens. You can't just lump it all together.

What's an accomplishment or point of pride in your career?

I have trained more than a dozen bartenders to become bar managers and have opened or reopened more than ten bars and restaurants in Arizona. I am proud to have had a direct role in shaping both the past and future of bartending in Tucson and the state as a whole.

Anything else on your mind?

Our bars aim to produce minimal/zero waste by limiting our range of perishable items like citrus fruits, and we aim to use all parts of the items, such as making cordials with juiced halves or pre-peeling garnishes. We also use preservation techniques such as infusions, dehydration, clarification, and syrup-making to make items last longer that would typically be available for only a limited time. We use fermentation to make vinegar from our leftover wines and overripe fruits.

Our goal has always been to showcase the best of our area and to do so sustainably. Our main inspiration for being sustainable was and continues to be the opportunity for unique flavors and the ability to show our guests the possibilities of what can be done with food and beverage without throwing things out.

BAD RAINS

C haparral is part of the native shrub creosote, which has been used for medicinal purposes for centuries. The amount used is small—5 grams of leaves infused per liter of bitters, for only an hour. Chaparral adds a great finishing touch for this bourbon cocktail.

||

GLASSWARE: Coupe glass

GARNISH: Chaparral-Infused Orange Bitters (see recipe)

- 1½ oz. | 45 ml Evan Williams Black Label bourbon
- ¾ oz. | 22.5 ml Dolin Rouge Vermouth
- ¾ oz. | 22.5 ml Amaro Montenegro
- ½ oz. | 15 ml Nixta Licor de Elote

1. Chill a coupe glass. Combine all of the ingredients in a mixing glass.
2. Add a fresh, large cube of ice; stir to combine and dilute for about 20 seconds.
3. Strain the cocktail into the chilled coupe.
4. Garnish with 2 spritzes of the infused orange bitters on the surface of the cocktail.

CHAPARRAL-INFUSED ORANGE BITTERS: Add 1 gram creosote leaves to 1 (5 oz.) bottle Regans' Orange Bitters No. 6 and allow the infusion to sit for 30 minutes. Strain the bitters into a spray bottle.

UGLY BUT HONEST

TOUGH LUCK CLUB
101 EAST PENNINGTON STREET, TUCSON

The quirky name of this spicy gin cocktail "comes from an inexpensive used car company that is just south of downtown," says beverage director Karl Góranowski. "I consider it my unofficial Tucson motto."

||

GLASSWARE: Collins glass
GARNISH: Mint, dehydrated lime wheel, candied ginger

- 1½ oz. | 45 ml Strawberry-Infused Gin (see recipe)
- ¾ oz. | 22.5 ml fresh lime juice
- ½ oz. | 15 ml ginger syrup
- ½ oz. | 15 ml Granada-Vallet Bitter Pomegranate Liqueur
- 3 oz. | 90 ml sparkling mineral water

1. Combine all of the ingredients, except for the sparkling water, in a cocktail shaker.
2. Add ice and shake vigorously for 15 seconds.
3. Open the shaker, add the sparkling water, and strain the cocktail into a collins glass with fresh ice.
4. Garnish with a generous bouquet of mint, a dehydrated lime wheel, candied ginger, and a straw.

STRAWBERRY-INFUSED GIN: In a large jar, combine 1 (750 ml) bottle of Bluecoat American Dry Gin and 10 to 12 organic strawberries, hulled and sliced. Allow the infusion to sit for 5 days then strain and rebottle.

MORE DOLLARS THAN SENSE

Bar director Karl Góranowski uses bacanora as a base in this drink, whose name hearkens back to dusty gunslingers in Arizona's Old West history. Bacanora, one of the lesser-known agave spirits, was outlawed in Mexico and made by underground distillers until the ban was repealed in 1992. Today, it's been granted Denomination of Origin and is made in thirty-five specific municipalities of Sonora.

GLASSWARE: Pilsner glass
GARNISH: Lime wedge, grapefruit peel, mint

- 1 oz. | 30 ml YooWE Bacanora
- 1 oz. | 30 ml El Dorado 3 Year Old Rum
- ½ oz. | 15 ml Giffard Blue Curaçao Liqueur
- ¾ oz. | 22.5 ml fresh lime juice
- ½ oz. | 15 ml Small Hand Foods Orgeat Syrup
- 1 oz. | 30 ml fresh grapefruit juice
- 2 dashes Regans' Orange Bitters No. 6

1. Combine all of the ingredients in a cocktail shaker and shake vigorously for 15 seconds.
2. Pour the cocktail into a pilsner glass filled with crushed ice.
3. Use a generous bouquet of mint in a grapefruit peel to garnish, along with a lime wedge and a straw.

FEARLESS VAMPIRE KILLER

Karl Góranowski has a penchant for unique names when it comes to his drinks, and this one is no exception. "This particular cocktail is named after a Bad Brains song," he says, "and I just think the idea of a fearless vampire killer is cool." He also points out that the Tucson-based Tough Luck Club has a punk rock, DIY attitude. "So I think this cocktail fits that vibe to a tee."

GLASSWARE: Large coupe glass
GARNISH: 2 dried lime wheels

- 1 oz. | 30 ml Mellow Corn Straight Corn Whiskey
- 1 oz. | 30 ml Suncliffe Arizona Gin
- ¾ oz. | 22.5 ml fresh lime juice
- ¾ oz. | 22.5 ml Fruitful Mission Fig Liqueur
- ¼ oz. | 7.5 ml Angostura bitters

1. Combine all of the ingredients in a cocktail shaker with ice and shake vigorously for 15 seconds.
2. Double-strain the cocktail into a large coupe glass.
3. Garnish with 2 dried lime wheels.

SAPIEN LANDING

PORTAL COCKTAILS
220 NORTH 4TH AVENUE, TUCSON

The back page of Portal Cocktails' menu warns (assures?) guests, "This world and everything in it will pass." It makes for good table conversation while sipping.

||

GLASSWARE: Rocks glass
GARNISH: Golden sage leaf

- 1½ oz. | 45 ml Coconut-Washed Pisco (see recipe)
- ¾ oz. | 22.5 ml Sage Pineapple Syrup (see recipe)
- ¾ oz. | 22.5 ml fresh lime juice
- ¼ oz. | 7.5 ml crème de violette

1. Combine all of the ingredients in a shaker with ice and shake.
2. Double-strain the cocktail over a large ice cube into a rocks glass.
3. Garnish with a leaf of golden sage.

COCONUT-WASHED PISCO: In a saucepan over low heat, liquify 100 grams coconut oil then pour it into a large jar. Pour 1 (750 ml) bottle of pisco into the jar, cover, and give it a hard shake. Infuse for 5 hours then put the jar in the freezer overnight. Using a knife, make a hole through the solidified fat. Pour the pisco through a fine-mesh strainer.

SAGE PINEAPPLE SYRUP: In a small saucepan over medium-low heat, combine 1 pineapple, skinned and chopped, with 2 cups water and 2 cups sugar and muddle the pineapple. Bring the mixture to a simmer, stirring until the sugar is dissolved, then remove from heat. Add fresh sage leaves and allow the syrup to cool completely.

BIRDIES UP

Portal Cocktails is located in the century-old Fourth Avenue district. The area abounds with indie shops that can occupy any vintage shopper's time, funky restaurants, and local organic ingredients. Portal Cocktails definitely fits in, with slick architecture and stained glass that draws you in.

GLASSWARE: Rocks glass
GARNISH: Brûléed banana slice

- 1½ oz. | 45 ml Brugal Añejo Rum
- ½ oz. | 15 ml Vecchio Magazzino Doganale Giocondo Caffe Cabaret Liqueur
- ½ oz. | 15 ml Giffard Banane du Brésil
- ¼ oz. | 7.5 ml Amaro Montenegro
- 2 dashes Angostura bitters

1. Combine all of the ingredients in a mixing glass with ice and stir.
2. Strain the cocktail over a large ice cube into a rocks glass.
3. Torch and brûlée a slice of banana on a skewer. Garnish by placing the skewer across the rim of the glass.

OBSIDIAN COOL

PORTAL COCKTAILS
220 NORTH 4TH AVENUE, TUCSON

This cocktail is listed under the dessert drinks section of the menu, as the description says that the taste is reminiscent of Reese's Pieces.

||

GLASSWARE: Rocks glass

GARNISH: Gold dust

- 1½ oz. | 45 ml Black Sesame–Infused Vodka (see recipe)
- ½ oz. | 15 ml Black Sesame Syrup (see recipe)
- ¼ oz. | 7.5 ml orgeat
- ¼ oz. | 7.5 ml Licor 43

1. Combine all of the ingredients in a shaker tin with ice and shake everything up with vigor.
2. Double-strain the cocktail over a large ice cube into a rocks glass.
3. Garnish by sprinkling gold dust on the ice cube.

BLACK SESAME–INFUSED VODKA: Toast ½ cup black sesame seeds. Combine the toasted seeds and 1 (750 ml) bottle of vodka in a large jar and infuse for 2 to 3 days. Fine-strain and rebottle.

BLACK SESAME SYRUP: Toast 1 cup black sesame seeds. In a small saucepan over medium heat, combine the toasted sesame seeds with 1 cup water and simmer for 10 to 20 minutes. Strain into a clean saucepan, using a wooden spoon to press the seeds, and combine with 1 cup sugar. Bring the mixture to a simmer, stirring until the sugar is dissolved. Allow the syrup to cool.

MANIFEST YOUR NATURE

PORTAL COCKTAILS
220 NORTH 4TH AVENUE, TUCSON

The ingredients to Manifest Your Nature read like something you would find in a pressed juice rather than a cocktail. However, the tequila and syrup provide the perfect balance to the sweetness of the carrot and richness of the beets. If you were manifesting the need for a fun new cocktail in your life, it's here.

॥

GLASSWARE: Collins glass
GARNISH: Sprig of dill, orange peel

- 1½ oz. | 45 ml Tequila Ocho Plata
- 1 oz. | 30 ml beet puree
- ¾ oz. | 22.5 ml fresh lime juice
- ½ oz. | 15 ml carrot juice
- ½ oz. | 15 ml Demerara Simple Syrup (see recipe on page 20)
- 2 dashes celery bitters

1. Combine all of the ingredients in a shaker tin with ice and shake everything up.
2. Strain the cocktail over crushed ice into a collins glass.
3. Garnish with a bright sprig of dill and an orange peel twist.

CENTRAL PHOENIX

JAMMIE DODGER

HASTA LA VISTA, BERRY!

PLOT TWIST

MIDNIGHT SNACK

CONVERSATION
STARTER

RED CURRANT FIX

DAIQURRY

ROSÉ ALL DAY

GARNET GURU

SOUK SAZERAC

THE DREAMTIME

ELOTE MODE

ESPIRITU DE CAFÉ

LECHE DE PISTACHIO

ROSEMARY'S OFRENDA

YUKI-ONNA

HAKUTAKU

FROM PHOENIX, WITH
LOVE

MEZCAL EXPERIENCE

DESERT DONKEY

DRUNKEN VIETNAMESE
COFFEE

KONOHA SOUR

LEMONGRASS SWIZZLE

DRUKEN WIFEY

LEAN LIKE A CHINOLA

NEWTON'S FIG

TUCSON SOUR

WHITE TAI

WHERE THERE'S SMOKE

SONORAN KATANA

HIDDEN ISLAND

Metropolitan Phoenix is massive, but Phoenix itself is no joke. Geographically, it is bigger than Los Angeles. In Central Phoenix are areas like Uptown, Melrose District, and Downtown, which has its own sub-neighborhoods like Roosevelt Row and more. And while one could enjoy a full night in any one of these locales, Phoenicians also don't think twice about traversing fifteen to thirty minutes to get to another area for a specific bar or restaurant (we're used to significant commutes here). In that way, the city flows together from neighborhood to neighborhood.

BITTER & TWISTED COCKTAIL PARLOUR

Ironically located in the former headquarters of Arizona Prohibition, Bitter & Twisted Cocktail Parlour occupies the Luhrs building in nearly the very center of the city. It's fitting that a bar of such caliber now calls the building, built in 1929 as another superb example of art deco design, home.

Opened in May 2014, Bitter & Twisted rapidly racked up the awards, being recognized locally and nationally for its drink selections and overall vibe. The bar hasn't looked back since, constantly refreshing its large and inventive menu, which has garnered its own awards thanks to artfully creative design and whimsical themes.

The bar interior has murals and an elegant backbar to draw the eye but not distract from the well-presented drinks in front of you. What's served here is impossible to ignore. Funky, unexpected, sometimes surprisingly simple and occasionally outlandish, this is not the type of place to order your usual classic cocktail—but even if you did, it would probably be one of the best versions you've ever had. Mixologist Ross Simon and his team pay attention to the details, including crafting their own infusions, syrups, and ice in-house. One of the Top 10 nominees in the World's Best Cocktail Menu category for the 2024 Tales of the Cocktail Foundation Spirited Awards, the impact Bitter & Twisted has had on the cocktail culture of this city, by showing Phoenicians they could drink better, is undeniable.

JAMMIE DODGER

BITTER & TWISTED COCKTAIL PARLOUR
1 WEST JEFFERSON STREET, PHOENIX

For those who don't know, a Jammie Dodger is a jam-filled short-bread sandwich biscuit (tea cookie) from the United Kingdom. The peanut butter cachaça, combined with the strawberry rhubarb syrup, brings to mind a boozy PB&J with a little treat on the side. And if you don't want to fly across the pond to pick up a pack of Jammie Dodgers for the garnish, they are available on Amazon.

GLASSWARE: Double rocks glass
GARNISH: Mini Jammie Dodger biscuit, brioche spray

- 2 oz. | 60 ml Peanut Butter Cachaça (see recipe)
- ¼ oz. | 7.5 ml Strawberry Rhubarb Syrup (see recipe)
- 2 drops 20% Saline Solution (see recipe on page 20)
- 4 to 5 drops Citric & Malic Acid Solution (see recipe)

1. Combine all of the ingredients in a mixing glass with ice and stir it up.
2. Strain the cocktail into the double rocks glass over a 2-inch-by-2-inch ice cube.
3. Garnish with a spritz of brioche spray and a mini Jammie Dodger biscuit.

PEANUT BUTTER CACHAÇA: Add 3 tablespoons unrefined, expeller-pressed roasted peanut oil to 1 (750 ml) bottle of Novo Fogo Silver Cachaça. Keep the bottle in the freezer for 24 hours. Quickly strain off the fats through a coffee filter.

STRAWBERRY RHUBARB SYRUP: In a saucepan over medium-low heat, combine 1 cup water and 1 cup sugar and bring to a simmer, stirring until the sugar is dissolved. Add 1 cup chopped strawberries and 1 cup chopped rhubarb, and continue to simmer until the fruits break down, about 10 to 15 minutes. Allow the syrup to cool and strain.

CITRIC & MALIC ACID SOLUTION: In a container, combine 2 ml citric acid, 2 ml malic acid, and 2½ oz. (75 ml) filtered water and stir until the powders are dissolved.

HASTA LA VISTA, BERRY!

BITTER & TWISTED COCKTAIL PARLOUR
1 WEST JEFFERSON STREET, PHOENIX

Hasta La Vista, Berry! is a great starter cocktail for an evening out at Bitter & Twisted or before heading into the heart of Phoenix. The bar sits right by the Footprint Center, home of the Phoenix Suns and Mercury and many a rocking concert.

GLASSWARE: Wineglass
GARNISH: Sprigs of red feather plants like celosia

- 1 oz | 30 ml Triple-Berry Shrub (see recipe)
- ¾ oz. | 22.5 ml mezcal
- ½ oz. | 15 ml Martini & Rossi Riserva Speciale Bitter Liqueur
- ½ oz. | 15 ml Ramazzotti Aperitivo Rosato
- 2 oz | 60 ml prosecco, to top
- 1 oz. | 30 ml club soda, to top

1. Combine all of the ingredients, except for the prosecco and club soda, in a mixing glass with ice and stir it up.
2. Strain the cocktail into a wineglass over cubes of ice.
3. Top it off with prosecco and the club soda, and garnish with celosia.

TRIPLE-BERRY SHRUB: Combine 1 cup blueberries, 1 cup blackberries, and 1 cup raspberries in a large container and mash the fruits a bit. Transfer the fruits to a large, clean jar. Add 3 cups sugar and stir. Allow the mixture to rest for 48 hours at room temperature, shaking or stirring occasionally. Strain the juice through a fine-mesh strainer and/or cheesecloth, using a wooden spoon to press as much juices as possible from the fruit. In a clean bottle or jar, combine the juice with apple cider vinegar or a wine vinegar, to taste (up to a 1:1 ratio by volume) and keep it in the refrigerator.

PLOT TWIST

Fresh pineapple juice, lime juice, and luscious plantain syrup unite in this recipe for a tropical adventure. Combined with the exotic blend of rum and Maker's Mark 46 plus the warmth of the Hamilton Jamaican Pimento Dram Liqueur, and it's like you're sitting on a sunny, sandy beach . . . even in landlocked Arizona.

GLASSWARE: Tiki glass

GARNISH: Plantain chips, mint, nutmeg

- 1½ oz. | 45 ml Rum-Bourbon Blend (see recipe)
- ½ oz. | 15 ml Hamilton Jamaican Pimento Dram Liqueur
- 1½ oz. | 45 ml pineapple juice
- ½ oz. | 15 ml fresh lime juice
- ¾ oz. | 22.5 ml Plantain Syrup (see recipe)

1. Combine all of the ingredients in a mixing glass and stir it up.
2. Use a spindle or immersion blender to blend up the ingredients until slightly frothy.
3. Pour the cocktail into a tiki glass over crushed ice. Use a fistful of mint as a garnish on top, along with a few plantain chips. Grate a touch of fresh nutmeg over the top.

PLANTAIN SYRUP: First, make Simple Syrup (see recipe on page 20), and while the syrup is cooking, add 1 cup chopped ripe plantain. Over low heat, simmer for 5 to 10 minutes. Allow the syrup to cool then strain, using a wooden spoon to press liquid from the plantain.

RUM-BOURBON BLEND: In a glass bottle or jar, combine Maker's Mark 46 and a rum of your choice in a one-to-one ratio.

ROSS SIMON, BITTER & TWISTED COCKTAIL PARLOUR, LITTLE RITUALS

In 2005, native Scotsman Ross Simon left the UK for Arizona with the idea of Bitter & Twisted in mind, looking to implement what he had experienced working in London here in the Valley. At first, he found little support for his concept. In order to change people's minds, Simon set about working with the few other like-minded individuals in town on an education campaign.

He co-founded the Phoenix Chapter of the United States Bartenders' Guild to help build up the bartending community. Simon also was a co-founder of Arizona Cocktail Weekend, a yearly celebration of spirits in the community that started as a way to increase cocktail awareness and education for consumers. In 2014, nine years after arriving in the States, Simon launched Bitter & Twisted Cocktail Parlour. It didn't immediately click. "If you read articles from back then," he explains, "writers still didn't understand what we were trying to do. So right out of the gate, we were still trying to win over hearts and minds and convince people that this was a feasible thing."

Eventually, people did understand what Simon and his peers were doing, as evidenced not only by the explosion of cocktail bars and lounges in Phoenix but also by the massive mainstream success of Arizona Cocktail Weekend. In the early 2000s, events like this were somewhat unthinkable; now it's one of the hottest tickets in town. In addition to Bitter & Twisted, Simon co-owns Little Rituals and has been involved with several other cocktail concepts around Phoenix, all while garnering numerous awards and accolades for his work, including, most recently, being named a Top 10 nominee in both the World's Best Cocktail Menu category (Bitter & Twisted) and the Best U.S. Hotel Bar category (Little Ritual) for the 2024 Tales of the Cocktail Foundation Spirited Awards. More importantly, he never gave up on Phoenix or the vision that we could have an amazing cocktail scene.

MIDNIGHT SNACK

LITTLE RITUALS

132 SOUTH CENTRAL AVENUE, 4TH FLOOR, PHOENIX

Complex, rich, and sultry, this cocktail blends nuts and umami in a strikingly effective way to create a lengthy and complex sipping experience. The black pepper praline helps tie all of the elements together and provides the snack portion of Midnight Snack.

GLASSWARE: Rocks glass

GARNISH: Black Pepper Praline (see recipe)

- 1½ oz. | 45 ml Shiitake-Infused Whiskey (see recipe)
- ¾ oz. | 22.5 ml Cardamaro
- ¾ oz. | 22.5 ml Vicario Nocino Walnut Liqueur
- 1 barspoon Reisetbauer Carrot Eau de Vie
- 2 dashes fennel bitters
- Lemon peel, to express

1. Chill a rocks glass. Combine all of the ingredients, except for the lemon peel, in a mixing glass with cracked and cubed ice and stir well.
2. Strain the cocktail over a large ice cube into the chilled rocks glass.
3. Express a lemon peel over the drink then discard it, and garnish with a Black Pepper Praline.

SHIITAKE-INFUSED WHISKEY: In a glass jar, combine 5 oz. Rittenhouse Straight Rye Whisky with 1 oz. dried shiitake mushrooms. Let the infusion sit for 12 hours. Carefully strain the whiskey through a double coffee filter.

BLACK PEPPER PRALINES: In a large saucepan, combine 450 grams granulated sugar, 450 grams light brown sugar, 360 grams heavy cream (40% butterfat), and 100 grams unsalted butter. Using a candy thermometer and a rubber spatula, heat the mixture over medium-high heat until it reaches a temperature of 240°F, being sure not to let the sugar scorch to the bottom of the pan. At this point, it will be boiling. When it reaches 240°F, remove the pan from heat and add 450 grams walnut halves and pieces, 1 gram baking soda, 6 grams kosher salt, 10 grams organic vanilla bean paste, and 40 grams ground black pepper. Mix until the mixture begins to thicken slightly, but be careful not to overmix and make it too thick. When the mixture is about 180°F, start spooning out spoonfuls on parchment paper and, while still hot, place a half walnut on the top of each cooling spoonful.

CONVERSATION STARTER

LITTLE RITUALS
132 SOUTH CENTRAL AVE, 4TH FLOOR, PHOENIX

"This gateway cocktail into the bitter world blends a classic Sour with an Italian aperitivo presentation for an irresistible crowd-pleaser," says Aaron DeFeo, co-owner of Little Rituals and a nationally acclaimed mixologist. He puts serious work into the Strawberry-Rhubarb Syrup, demonstrating how paying attention to the small details is one of the reasons Little Rituals is at the top of the Arizona cocktail game.

GLASSWARE: Large goblet
GARNISH: Pineapple frond, dehydrated lemon wheel

- 1½ oz. | 45 ml rye-based vodka
- 1 oz. | 30 ml fresh lemon juice
- 1 oz. | 30 ml fresh pineapple juice
- ¾ oz. | 22.5 ml Strawberry-Rhubarb Syrup (see recipe)
- ½ oz. | 15 ml Select Aperitivo

1. Chill a goblet. Combine all of the ingredients in a cocktail shaker with a small amount of pebble ice and shake hard (whip-shake).

2. Pour the frothy mixture into the chilled goblet. Top with ice.

3. Garnish with a pineapple frond and a dehydrated lemon wheel.

STRAWBERRY-RHUBARB SYRUP: In a large container, combine 1 liter Monin Strawberry Syrup, 1 liter wildflower honey-and-water mixture (1:1 ratio water to honey), 250 grams strawberries, 1 oz. rhubarb bitters, 5 grams citric acid, and 1 gram ascorbic acid. Vacuum seal and sous vide at 140°F for 2 hours. Chill the syrup down in an ice bath, then strain it through a conical mesh strainer and then a cheesecloth or paper filter before bottling.

RED CURRANT FIX

LITTLE RITUALS
132 SOUTH CENTRAL AVENUE, 4TH FLOOR, PHOENIX

Full of tart red berries and citrus, this lively, balanced, fruit-forward cocktail transforms simple into extraordinary. With some resemblance to a sangria, it is perfect for a long, hot summer day. The redcurrants are a lovely and unexpected touch, as they're popular throughout Europe but not used quite as much in the United States.

GLASSWARE: 13 oz. glass

GARNISH: Banana leaf, red currants, pink peppercorns, powdered sugar

---

- 1½ oz. | 45 ml Tanqueray N° Ten Gin
- ¾ oz. | 22.5 ml Yuzu and Lemon Juice Blend (see recipe)
- ¾ oz. | 22.5 ml Cocchi Americano
- ¾ oz. | 22.5 ml Red Currant Cordial (see recipe)

1. Combine all of the ingredients in a cocktail shaker and whip-shake (add a small amount of pebble ice and shake quickly).
2. Dump the contents into a 13 oz. glass, then pack it to the brim with additional ice. This particular cocktail benefits from extra dilution.
3. To garnish, wrap the banana leaf into a cone and tuck it into the side of the glass. Place red currants in the cone and lightly dust them with powdered sugar. Add some pink peppercorns to the top of the glass.

YUZU AND LEMON JUICE BLEND: In a container, mix yuzu juice and lemon juice in a 1:3 ratio.

RED CURRANT CORDIAL: In a saucepan, combine 600 grams (600 ml) filtered water and 300 grams red currants and bring the mixture to a boil. Add 750 grams cane sugar, 12 grams citric acid, and 5 grams crushed pink peppercorns, and reduce the heat. Simmer for 1 minute, then turn off the heat and stir. Allow the cordial to cool for 30 minutes then strain.

DAIQURRY

LITTLE RITUALS
132 SOUTH CENTRAL AVENUE, 4TH FLOOR, PHOENIX

There are few pleasures more universally enjoyable in the cocktail world than a Daiquiri," says Little Rituals co-owner Aaron DeFeo. "This puts an unexpected twist on the classic by adding a spiced savory element that keeps you going back in for additional sips. Definitely a fresh, bright, vibrant, and exotic cocktail." For the rum, you can use any blended island rum.

GLASSWARE: Coupe glass
GARNISH: Curry leaf, colored Sichuan oil

- 1½ oz. | 45 ml Planteray 3 Stars Rum
- 1 oz. | 30 ml fresh lime juice
- ¾ oz. | 22.5 ml Yellow Curry Syrup (see recipe)
- ½ oz. | 15 ml Yellow Chartreuse

1. Chill a coupe glass. Combine all of the ingredients in a cocktail shaker and shake hard with cold, hard ice.
2. Double-strain the cocktail into the chilled coupe.
3. Garnish with a curry leaf and drops of Sichuan pepper oil. To color, mix the oil with powder color or oil-soluble color; don't use regular food coloring. Use a medicine dropper to place drops of the oil on the top of the drink.

YELLOW CURRY SYRUP: In a small saucepan over medium-low heat, combine 1 cup water with ½ cup sugar and ½ cup Thai yellow curry powder and stir until the solids are dissolved.

ROSÉ ALL DAY

CARCARA
320 NORTH 3RD STREET, PHOENIX

We highlight citrus in this cocktail, one of the 5 Cs of Arizona," says top mixologist Tim Smith. Rosé All Day is "a perfect and refreshing cocktail to sip and savor in the dry heat of Arizona."

GLASSWARE: Bordeaux wineglass
GARNISH: Orange slices, fresh strawberries

- 4 oz. | 120 ml Chateau Ste. Michelle Altered Dimension Rosé
- ½ oz. | 15 ml fresh lemon juice
- ½ oz. | 15 ml peach schnapps
- ½ oz. | 15 ml strawberry puree
- Fever-Tree Ginger Beer, to top

1. Combine all of the ingredients, except for the ginger beer, in a cocktail shaker and shake.
2. Pour the cocktail into a Bordeaux wineglass and add half a scoop of ice.
3. Top with ginger beer and garnish with orange slices and fresh strawberries.

MAXWELL BERLIN, QUARTZ BAR AND THE CAVE

What's your favorite cocktail to make?
Caipirinhas with lots of tropical fruits.

How did you get interested in cocktails and mixology?
I'm a lover of food and travel. I've spent my life globe-trotting, looking for exotic ingredients and stories to share with my guests. I started my career in fine dining and working with some of the best ingredients, wines, and spirits in the world. Mixology came naturally to me as a way to express my culinary creativity.

What influences you as a mixologist?
My passion in life is to wander markets around the world to find the most interesting and unique ingredients to mix into my cocktails. I always have an ear to the ground, traveling to some of the world's best bars and restaurants looking for new trends, techniques, and styles of cocktails.

How do you draw inspiration from your local area when creating new drinks? And what do you admire about Phoenix's cocktail culture?
Phoenix is truly a gem of a city. We have a diverse and colorful fabric of restaurants, markets, cultural festivities, and artists coming together to create somewhere uniquely us. I'm so proud of where we've come from as a city and so excited to be a part of where we are going. We now have some of the best bars in the world that span the spectrum from rocking tiki dive bars with live music to fancy cocktail bars with the most creative cocktails in the country. We've moved beyond retirees and cowboys, and now we are a true cosmopolitan city, smack-dab in the desert.

What are some underrated ingredients you love to use and why?
First and foremost is salt. You wouldn't make dinner without it; why would you skip it in a cocktail? I'm also notorious for using lots of exotic Asian ingredients, including my signature item, fish sauce. Fish

sauce adds depth and umami that lends itself perfectly to almost any style of cocktail. Utilizing unusual ingredients can transport the imbiber to faraway places without ever leaving the comfort of our bar.

What's one thing about Phoenix that you think people don't understand or is misconstrued?

We aren't just chains and strip malls. Don't get me wrong, I do love me a strip mall hole-in-the-wall, but we now have creative people making a cornucopia of delicious bites and sips. Phoenix is known for our Thai food, pizza, creative cocktails, and so much more. Come visit us soon!

What's an accomplishment or point of pride in your career?

I've been blessed with a multitude of accolades, a James Beard nomination, competition wins, and so much more, but what I'm most proud of is the family I've built in this beautiful city and beyond. I now travel the country spreading the word that Arizona is a culinary force to be reckoned with.

Any final thoughts?

Don't skip out on other cities here in Arizona. Tucson is a culinary tour de force, Bisbee is quirky, and Payson is gorgeous. We have a world wonder in the Grand Canyon, and we are worth exploring.

GARNET GURU

Instead of a summer Spritz or Sangria, try the Garnet Guru! This sparkling recipe speaks to Quartz's birthstone-based menu that incorporates a different cocktail for each of the twelve birthstones. Note that *himbeergeist* refers to made-in-(usually) Germany raspberry brandy, of which several brands are available.

GLASSWARE: Wineglass

- ¾ oz. | 22.5 ml fresh lemon juice
- ¾ oz. | 22.5 ml grenadine
- ½ oz. | 15 ml Granada-Vallet Bitter Pomegranate Liqueur
- ½ oz. | 15 ml Dolin Rouge Vermouth

- ½ oz. | 15 ml himbeergeist
- 2 dashes crème de violette
- 1½ oz. | 45 ml Scarpetta Frico Lambrusco, to top
- Lemon peel, to express

1. Chill a wineglass. Combine all of the ingredients, except for the sparkling wine and lemon peel, in a cocktail shaker with ice and shake until chilled.
2. Strain the cocktail over a large ice ball into the chilled wineglass.
3. Top with the wine.
4. Express a lemon peel over the cocktail then discard.

SOUK SAZERAC

QUARTZ
341 WEST VAN BUREN STREET, SUITE B, PHOENIX

Mixologist Maxwell Berlin has used his travels to influence the cocktails he creates, which leads to delights like the Souk Sazerac. It includes an ingredient that is familiar to the desert, although perhaps not our Sonoran one—camel fat. Fat-washing is a technique that involves freezing spirits with fat before straining through a cheesecloth. In this case, the fat is from a camel and helps bolster this drinkable journey to the Middle East. If you can't source camel fat, substitute with your preferred fat.

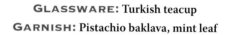

GLASSWARE: Turkish teacup
GARNISH: Pistachio baklava, mint leaf

- 1 oz. | 30 ml Camel Fat– Washed Overproof Rye Whiskey (see recipe)
- 1 oz. | 30 ml Brancamenta
- 3 dashes Angostura bitters
- Absinthe, to spritz
- Lemon peel, to express

1. Combine the whiskey, mint amaro, and bitters in a chilled mixing glass over fresh ice and stir until chilled.
2. Strain the cocktail into a Turkish teacup and add a spritz of absinthe, then express a lemon peel overtop and discard the peel.
3. Garnish with a mint leaf and piece of pistachio baklava on the side.

CAMEL FAT–WASHED OVERPROOF RYE WHISKEY: Render camel fat by cooking it in a saucepan over a low heat until it becomes liquified. Add the rendered fat to 1 (750 ml) bottle of overproof rye then chill the rye in the freezer overnight. The fat will solidify on top of the alcohol, making it easier to remove. Strain the rye through a cheesecloth or coffee filter.

THE DREAMTIME

This cocktail is comfortingly reminiscent of a certain sleepy bear's evening tea, brightened with a hit of eucalyptus. Quartz takes advantage of Arizona's wild botanicals to infuse the gins they use.

GLASSWARE: Blown glass vessel or collins glass
GARNISH: Eucalyptus honeycomb candy

- 1½ oz. | 45 ml AZ Botanicals–Infused Gin (see recipe)
- ½ oz. | 15 ml mezcal pechuga de conejo
- ¾ oz. | 22.5 ml blood orange syrup
- ¾ oz. | 22.5 ml Manuka Honey Syrup (see recipe on page 20)
- ¾ oz. | 22.5 ml lemon myrtle tea
- ¾ oz. | 22.5 ml fresh lemon juice
- 3 dashes eucalyptus bitters
- Ginger beer, to top

1. Chill a glass. Combine all of the ingredients, except for the ginger beer, in a cocktail shaker with ice and give that shaker a quick, good shake.

2. Strain the cocktail into the chilled glass over fresh pebble ice.

3. Top with ginger beer and garnish with the honeycomb candy.

AZ BOTANICALS–INFUSED GIN: Infuse 1 (750 ml) bottle of Suncliffe Arizona Gin with foraged Arizona botanicals for 1 to 3 days and strain.

DEREK MATTSON, BARCOA AGAVERIA

What's your favorite drink?

Shot and a beer. Any light beer, preferably a Mexican lager, and a shot of palmilla, which is sotol from the Mexican state of Sonora.

How did you get interested in cocktails and mixology?

I grew up in a chaotic household and often went to friends' houses to get away. Now I'm used to being around chaotic energy. Growing up, I wanted to be an anthropologist to learn about human nature and our relationship with the world around us, but then I found out there's no money in anthropology. So I took up bartending to make money and found that I thrived in that chaotic environment. And bartending led me to a love for agave spirits, where we're talking about plants and botany.

What influences you as a mixologist?

The iceberg effect—that endless pursuit of knowledge behind cocktails, the spirits, and how to creatively make things that are both original and taste good. I love reading about spirits and cocktails, so I'm most influenced by whatever I'm reading at the time. Right now, it's *The Essential Tequila & Mezcal Companion* by Tess Rose Lampert, one of the pioneers in the world of agave spirits.

How do you draw inspiration from your local area?

The history behind the land and the cultures that came before us and how they made these spirits is so intriguing. For instance, we live in the Sonoran desert; bacanora is a type of mezcal made in the state of Sonora, which sits right below us. So naturally, the spirit tastes like something made in our terroir. I love figuring out how to make something taste "Sonoran" with this spirit or palmilla. How humans interact with these plants and the spirits that come from them is fascinating to me.

What do you find unique about Arizona's cocktail culture?

A lot of people still don't know much about agave spirits here in Arizona, even with our proximity to Mexico. But this gives me the opportunity to educate guests. I'm a native Arizonan, so it's fulfilling to tell the stories of our geographical neighbor and the cultural history behind the spirits that come from there.

What are some underrated ingredients you love to use and why?

Cheese and yogurt. I tend to favor spirits that have a lactic quality, which typically results from a long fermentation. This is where the spirit can develop some funky flavors. Sometimes, when building a cocktail, you can skip fat washing for that lactic effect and just grab a bottle of raicilla.

But I do love fat washing with yogurt and trying to recreate cheesy flavors. In cocktails, this can make people feel uncomfortable and force them out of their comfort zone. For instance, I recently made a cocktail that had hibiscus green tea–infused Arette Reposado Tequila that was then fat washed with cream cheese. The cocktail was built with Bulleit Bourbon, Kalani Coconut Liqueur, and Licor 43 before clarifying with coconut and soy milk. A couple dashes of a lactic solution added roundness and creaminess. Then it was carbonated. It was wild. We'll likely feature a version of it at BARCOA soon.

What's one thing about Arizona that you think people don't understand or is misconstrued?

That we're a state of just Mexican food. We have great Thai, French, Italian—Arizona's strength is that it's a melting pot. Our cocktail scene has Top 50 bars, places that play on tiki or escapism, and true modern innovators. I think people will learn that Arizona is not just on the outskirts anymore.

What's an accomplishment or point of pride in your career?

I recently won a cocktail competition with Homeward Bound, which raises money to help people out of the cycle of homelessness. We were required to use a vodka and rosé wine, so my cocktail featured Greek yogurt fat-washed Arizona Distilling vodka, a strawberry rosé wine cordial, and mint foam.

ELOTE MODE

BARCOA AGAVERIA
829 NORTH 1ST AVENUE, PHOENIX

The corn eaten around the world originated in Mexico nearly ten thousand years ago," explains bartender Nick Fiorini. "The Old Fashioned is also one of the first cocktails in print, so naturally we decided a corn Old Fashioned would be a staple here at BARCOA and will remain on the menu indefinitely."

GLASSWARE: Rocks glass
GARNISH: Dried corn husk tied around the glass, orange peel

- 1 oz. | 30 ml Vago Elote
- 1 oz. | 30 ml Abasolo El Whisky De Mexico
- ¼ oz. | 7.5 ml Nixta Licor de Elote

- ¼ oz. | 7.5 ml Piloncillo Syrup (see recipe)
- 2 dashes Angostura bitters
- 2 dashes Angostura orange bitters

1. Combine all of the ingredients in a mixing glass and stir.
2. Pour the cocktail over a large-format ice cube.
3. To garnish, wrap the dried corn husk around the glass and tie it, then express the orange peel over the drink and drop it in between the glass and the ice cube.

PILONCILLO SYRUP: In a saucepan over low heat, combine 2 cups piloncillo and 1 cup water, and stir until the piloncillo is dissolved. Allow the syrup to cool.

ESPIRITU DE CAFÉ

BARCOA AGAVERIA
829 NORTH 1ST AVENUE, PHOENIX

Bartenders Jourdain Blanchette and Nick Fiorini make their own coffee-infused liqueur. It makes all the difference for this feisty drink that was inspired by a Carajillo through the lens of an Espresso Martini, while only using spirits from Mexico.

GLASSWARE: Coupe glass

GARNISH: Vegan Chocolate Cream (see recipe), cinnamon

- 1 oz. | 30 ml Azuñia Reposado Organic Tequila
- 1 oz. | 30 ml Coffee-Infused Licor 43 (see recipe)
- ½ oz. | 15 ml Casa D'Aristi Narano Bitter Orange Liqueur
- ½ oz. | 15 ml Kalani Coconut Liqueur

1. Combine all of the ingredients in a mixing glass and add ice.
2. Stir up and strain into a coupe glass.
3. Garnish with the cream and a dusting of cinnamon.

COFFEE-INFUSED LICOR 43: Combine 1 (750 ml) bottle of Licor 43 with 1 cup ground coffee. After 48 hours, strain the liqueur through a coffee filter and rebottle.

VEGAN CHOCOLATE CREAM: Combine dairy-free heavy cream and white crème de cocoa in a 2:1 ratio of and shake until incorporated.

LECHE DE PISTACHIO

BARCOA AGAVERIA
829 NORTH 1ST AVENUE, PHOENIX

This drink is inspired by a drink you get at Ranch Market, a local Mexican market. They have freshly made aguas frescas and I love getting the pistachio one when I shop there," says bartender Jourdain Blanchette. "I decided to replicate the drink for BARCOA but also wanted everyone to enjoy it regardless of food preferences or allergies."

||

GLASSWARE: Coupe glass
GARNISH: Pistachio Dust (see recipe)

- **2 oz. | 60 ml Pistachio Milk (see recipe)**
- **1½ oz. | 45 ml Mezcal El Silencio Espadín**
- **½ oz. | 15 ml fresh lime juice**
- **½ oz. | 15 ml Piloncillo Syrup (see recipe on 118)**
- **6 drops 20% Saline Solution (see recipe on page 20)**

1. Combine all of the ingredients in a cocktail shaker, add ice, and shake.
2. Double-strain the cocktail into a coupe.
3. Garnish the side of the glass with the Pistachio Dust.

PISTACHIO MILK: In a container, combine 32 oz. coconut milk, 1 cup sugar, ½ oz. nut-free pistachio extract, and 2 drops of green food coloring. Whisk until the sugar is completely dissolved.

122 — ARIZONA COCKTAILS

PISTACHIO DUST: Blend 1 cup unshelled pistachios in a food processor for 3 to 5 minutes.

ROSEMARY'S OFRENDA

BARCOA AGAVERIA
829 NORTH IST AVENUE, PHOENIX

A ccording to bartender Grant Gardner, adding a sweet fruit into the mezcal provides a nice note to the long, spicy, peppery finish and slight lactic acid to this type of agave. One of the things that makes BARCOA unique is their knowledge and representation for agave spirits in all forms. It's a must-visit for anyone looking to expand beyond the world of tequila.

||

GLASSWARE: Short-stemmed square goblet
GARNISH: Lemon peel, rosemary sprig

- 1½ oz. | 45 ml Peach-Infused Mezcal (see recipe)
- 1 oz. | 30 ml fresh lemon juice
- ½ oz. | 15 ml Ancho Reyes Verde Chile Poblano Liqueur
- ½ oz. | 15 ml peach puree

1. Combine all of the ingredients in a cocktail shaker with ice and shake.
2. Strain the cocktail over fresh ice into a goblet.
3. Garnish with a lemon peel and sprig of fresh rosemary.

PEACH-INFUSED MEZCAL: In a large glass jar, combine 1½ cups frozen organic peaches with 1 (750 ml) bottle of IZO Cenizo Mezcal and allow the infusion to sit for 2 to 3 days. Strain and rebottle.

YUKI-ONNA

SAKE HAUS
214 EAST ROOSEVELT STREET, PHOENIX

Mixologist DeAndre' Rodriguez's spicy gin is the perfect base for this coconutty cocktail with a bite.

GLASSWARE: Collins glass
GARNISH: Mint, Thai chile, toasted coconut flake

- 1½ oz. | 45 ml Haus Infused Thai Chile Roku Gin (see recipe)
- ¾ oz. | 22.5 ml fresh lime juice
- ½ oz. | 15 ml Simple Syrup (see recipe on page 20)
- ½ oz. | 15 ml raspberry puree
- ½ oz. | 15 ml Liquid Alchemist Coconut Cocktail Syrup
- ½ oz. | 15 ml mezcal
- ¼ oz. | 7.5 ml Aperol

1. Combine all of the ingredients in a cocktail shaker with ice and shake.
2. Dirty-dump (don't strain) the cocktail into a collins glass.
3. Garnish with mint, a Thai chile, and a toasted coconut flake.

HAUS INFUSED THAI CHILE ROKU GIN: Combine 34 oz. (1,000 ml) Roku Gin and 9 Thai chiles, butterflied, in a container and let the mixture marinate for 48 hours. Strain the gin and discard the peppers.

HAKUTAKU

SAKE HAUS
214 EAST ROOSEVELT STREET, PHOENIX

In Japanese lore, a *hakutaku* is a mythical, bull-like beast deity with a third eye. According to legend, a hakutaku once helped the emperor of China learn how to defeat evil supernatural beings, and now hakutaku are considered a good luck charm. Ordering the Hakutaku at Sake Haus may or may not bring good luck, but it's worth a try.

GLASSWARE: Collins glass
GARNISH: Mint, cucumber ribbon, black pepper

- 1½ oz. | 45 ml Haku Vodka
- ¾ oz. | 25 ml Fruitful Papaya Liqueur
- ¾ oz. | 25 ml Simple Syrup (see recipe on page 20)
- ½ oz. | 15 ml fresh lemon juice
- ¼ oz. | 7.5 ml St-Germain Elderflower Liqueur
- Soda water, to top

1. Combine all of the ingredients, except for the soda water, in a cocktail shaker with ice and shake well.
2. Strain the cocktail over ice into a collins glass.
3. Top off with soda water.
4. Garnish with mint, a cucumber ribbon, and some black pepper.

FROM PHOENIX, WITH LOVE

SAKE HAUS
214 EAST ROOSEVELT STREET, PHOENIX

Sake Haus is just one example of the sushi gems that are tucked away around Phoenix. Raw fish in the desert comes across like an oxymoron, but the city has a beautiful and underrated Japanese dining scene. Sake Haus takes it a step further by presenting themselves as a spirit-forward sushi bar, embracing a strong cocktail menu and local sake to complement the killer food.

GLASSWARE: Rocks glass

GARNISH: Mint, dehydrated blood orange slice, dusting of cinnamon

- 1½ oz. | 45 ml Cenote Blanco Tequila
- ¾ oz. | 22.5 ml fresh lime juice
- ¾ oz. | 22.5 ml Demerara Simple Syrup (see recipe on page 20)
- ½ oz. | 15 ml Haus Infused Strawberry Campari (see recipe)
- ½ oz. | 15 ml passion fruit puree

1. Combine all of the ingredients in a cocktail shaker with ice and shake well.
2. Dirty-dump (don't strain) the cocktail into a rocks glass.
3. Garnish with a healthy portion of mint, a dehydrated slice of blood orange, and a generous dusting of cinnamon.

HAUS INFUSED STRAWBERRY CAMPARI: In a jar or other non-reactive container, combine 1 quart hulled and chopped strawberries with 1 (750 ml) bottle of Campari and let the infusion sit for 3 to 4 days. Strain and rebottle the Campari.

MEZCAL EXPERIENCE

PERSEPSHEN
4700 NORTH CENTRAL AVENUE, PHOENIX

Chef and co-owner Jason Dwight believes less is more as he replicates an experience often found in Mexico City. With a hearty pour of mezcal, he serves thirteen chili lime garlic grasshoppers, aka *sal de chapulín*, which is a common snack in Mexico to pair with the spirit, along with the chili larva worm salt, aka *sal de gusano*. Try ordering the special ingredients online to replicate the experience at Perepshen.

GLASSWARE: Copita and small rectangular plate
GARNISH: 13 chili garlic lime grasshoppers,
tangerine slice, chili larva worm salt

- **2 oz. | 60 ml Mezcal Carreño Espadín**

1. Place a copita in the center of a small rectangular plate then pour the mezcal into the copita.
2. Place the grasshoppers in a group to the left of the copita.
3. Place one tangerine slice to the right.
4. For the final flourish, sprinkle the slice with chili larva worm salt.

DESERT DONKEY

PERSEPSHEN
4700 NORTH CENTRAL AVENUE, PHOENIX

"Chug, enjoy, repeat!" says chef and co-owner Jason Dwight about this cocktail. Persepshen takes pride in making all of its ingredients in-house, including the jam and syrup for the Desert Donkey. The effort comes through in this bright and well-balanced drink.

‖

GLASSWARE: Porcelain enamel–coated metal cup or copper mug
GARNISH: Mint sprig, candied ginger

- 1½ oz. | 45 ml Canyon Diablo Desert Rain Gin
- 1½ oz. | 45 ml fresh lime juice
- 1 tablespoon | 15 ml strawberry-vanilla jam
- ½ oz. | 15 ml Ginger Syrup (see recipe)
- ½ oz. | 15 ml Mint Gastrique (see recipe)
- 6 to 8 oz. | 177 to 237 ml sparkling water, to top

1. Pack a mug full of ice.
2. Combine all of the ingredients, except for the sparkling water, in a cocktail shaker.
3. Add the sparkling water and shake vigorously.
4. Pour the cocktail into the mug then garnish with a mint sprig, piece of candied ginger, and serve with a straw.

GINGER SYRUP: In a saucepan over medium-low heat, combine 1 cup water and 1 cup sugar. Simmer, stirring until the sugar is dissolved. Add 1 cup peeled and sliced fresh ginger and continue to heat, bringing the syrup to a light boil. Cover, reduce the heat, and allow the syrup to simmer for about 15 minutes. Remove the pan from heat and allow the syrup to cool. Strain out the ginger, bottle the syrup, and keep it in the refrigerator.

MINT GASTRIQUE: In a small, heavy saucepan over medium-low heat, melt 1 cup sugar, stirring to ensure it doesn't burn. Slowly add ½ cup vinegar of your choice to deglaze the pot, stirring, and lower the heat. Simmer the mixture until it has reduced to a thick syrup consistency and add a small handful of mint leaves for the final 5 minutes. Strain.

DRUNKEN VIETNAMESE COFFEE

PERSEPSHEN
4700 NORTH CENTRAL AVENUE, PHOENIX

Co-owner and chef Jason Dwight says that this particular cocktail was inspired by dive-y Vietnamese restaurants. The homemade and organic sweetened condensed milk sums up an experience at this downtown restaurant and bar, where the team's goal is making sure everything presented to the customer is clean, local, organic, and sustainable, in a homey environment.

GLASSWARE: Coupette glass

GARNISH: Luxardo maraschino cherry on a pick

- 2 oz. | 60 ml Grand Canyon Diablo Bourbon Whiskey
- 1½ oz. | 45 ml Espresso Blue house coffee
- Dash white truffle bitters
- 1 oz. | 30 ml organic sweetened condensed milk
- ½ oz. | 15 ml Luxardo maraschino cherry syrup

1. Combine all of the ingredients in a cocktail shaker with a scoop of ice and shake everything up.
2. Strain the cocktail into a coupette.
3. Garnish with a Luxardo maraschino cherry on a pick.

KONOHA SOUR

ACROSS THE POND
4236 NORTH CENTRAL AVENUE, SUITE 101, PHOENIX

A shrub is used to bring some acidity to a cocktail, and in this case, Across The Pond is using the Japanese shiso leaf to help tie the drink into their sushi menu.

||

GLASSWARE: Rocks glass

GARNISH: Shiso leaf, Peychaud's bitters

- 1½ oz. | 45 ml pisco
- ¾ oz. | 22.5 ml Shisho Pomegranate Shrub (see recipe)
- ½ oz. | 15 ml Yellow Chartreuse
- ½ oz. | 15 ml fresh lemon juice
- ¼ oz. | 7.5 ml fresh lime juice
- 1 egg white
- 3 dashes orange bitters

1. Combine all of the ingredients in a cocktail shaker without ice and dry-shake to emulsify the egg white.
2. Add ice and wet-shake (shake normally).
3. Strain the cocktail into a rocks glass while vigorously tapping the strainer to remove any air bubbles from the egg white foam.
4. Garnish with a single shiso leaf and several drops of Peychaud's bitters, arranged artistically.

SHISHO POMEGRANATE SHRUB: Bring ½ cup sugar, 8 to 10 shiso leaves, and 1 (500 ml) bottle of pomegranate vinegar to a boil, then lower the heat and simmer, stirring, for 10 minutes. Allow the liquid to cool, then strain.

LEMONGRASS SWIZZLE

ACROSS THE POND
4236 NORTH CENTRAL AVENUE, SUITE 101, PHOENIX

The name Across The Pond may beckon images of a British pub, but here in Phoenix, it represents the other side of the world. Offering fresh and traditional sushi, Across The Pond's Japanese flavors carry over into the cocktail menu, a collaborative effort with local legend mixologist, Joshua James. You can substitute Tito's Handmade Vodka for the Monopolowa.

⫼

GLASSWARE: Collins glass

GARNISH: Cucumber tape

- 2 oz. | 60 ml Monopolowa
- 2 oz. | 60 ml Cucumber Water (see recipe)
- ½ oz. | 15 ml yuzu juice
- ¾ oz. | 22.5 ml Lemongrass Syrup (see recipe)
- ¼ oz. | 7.5 ml fresh lime juice

1. Combine all of the ingredients in a collins glass and fill the glass halfway with crushed ice.

2. Using a barspoon, agitate the ingredients and ice for 1 minute to mix and incorporate.

3. Top with more crushed ice and garnish with cucumber tape.

CUCUMBER WATER: Wash a cucumber and slice it into thin strips. Place the strips In a large glass jug, jar, or carafe, then top with ice and water and store in the refrigerator for 1 hour.

LEMONGRASS SYRUP: Prepare a lemongrass stalk by peeling its outer layer and discarding it, rolling the stalk to soften it, and then chopping it into small pieces. Combine the chopped lemongrass and 1 cup water in a small saucepan over medium-low heat and simmer, stirring occasionally, for about 10 minutes. Strain and combine the water with an equal amount of sugar and simmer, stirring until the sugar is dissolved. Allow the syrup to cool.

DRUNKEN WIFEY

MORA ITALIAN

The uniquely named Drunken Wifey uses mesquite honey to provide some of the sweet balance against the blanco tequila. Mesquite honey is native to the American Southwest, as it comes from bees using the sprawling mesquite trees that dot the desert. It has a naturally light and delicately floral flavor, which makes it the ideal pairing to the elderflower liqueur and limoncello.

GLASSWARE: Wineglass
GARNISH: Dehydrated lemon wheel, thyme sprigs

- Thick Simple Syrup (see recipe on page 20), for the rim
- Drunken Wifey Salt (see recipe), for the rim
- 2 oz. | 60 ml El Tequileño Blanco Tequila
- ½ oz. | 15 ml Fiorente Elderflower liqueur
- ½ oz. | 15 ml Mesquite Honey Simple Syrup (see recipe)
- ¼ oz. | 7.5 ml Simple Syrup (see recipe on page 20)
- ½ oz. | 15 ml limoncello
- 1½ oz. | 45 ml water
- ½ oz. | 15 ml fresh lemon juice

1. Paint the side of a wineglass with the Thick Simple Syrup then dip the glazed side of the glass in the Drunken Wifey Salt to create a strip on the side.
2. Build the drink, in the order of ingredients listed, in the wineglass.
3. Top with ice and garnish with a dehydrated lemon wheel and some thyme sprigs.

DRUNKEN WIFEY SALT: Combine Maldon Sea Salt Flakes, dehydrated lime zest, dehydrated lemon zest, dehydrated orange zest, a little touch of Aleppo pepper, and a sprinkle of edible flower petals.

MESQUITE HONEY SIMPLE SYRUP: Use mesquite honey to make Honey Syrup (see recipe on page 20).

LEAN LIKE A CHINOLA

MORA ITALIAN
5651 NORTH 7TH STREET, PHOENIX

The key to this cocktail is all in the "Campari sink," a technique where heavier syrups or liqueurs sink to the bottom of the glass regardless of when the rest of the drink is poured, creating a beautiful visual effect.

GLASSWARE: Rocks glass
GARNISH: Dehydrated pink pineapple wedge, passion fruit pearl boba

- ½ oz. | 15 ml Campari
- 1 oz. | 30 ml Espolòn Tequila Reposado
- ¾ oz. | 22.5 ml Chinola Passion Fruit Liqueur
- ¾ oz. | 22.5 ml fresh lime juice
- ½ oz. | 15 ml Montelobos Mezcal Espadín
- ½ oz. | 15 ml Heirloom Pineapple Amaro
- ½ oz. | 15 ml Basil Simple Syrup (see recipe)
- ¼ oz. | 7.5 ml pineapple juice

1. Sink the Campari into the glass first.
2. Combine the remaining ingredients in a cocktail shaker with ice and shake.
3. Strain the cocktail into the bucket glass slowly while making sure the Campari stays on the bottom.
4. Garnish with a dehydrated pink pineapple wedge and a handful of passion fruit pearl boba.

144 — ARIZONA COCKTAILS

BASIL SIMPLE SYRUP: In a small saucepan over medium-low heat, combine 1 cup water and 1 bunch fresh basil and simmer, stirring occasionally, for 10 to 15 minutes. Strain and combine the water with an equal amount of sugar and simmer, stirring until the sugar is dissolved. Allow the syrup to cool.

NEWTON'S FIG

TESOTA
300 WEST CAMELBACK ROAD, PHOENIX

This cocktail is named after The Newton, which is the mixed-use retail space on the heart of Camelback Road in Central Phoenix that Tesota helps anchor. Newton's Fig is one of Tesota's most popular cocktails, and it's easy to see why: the recipe is simple but comes with an unexpected twist of fig vodka. Try Figenza, which uses Mediterranean figs for its infusion and is available nationwide.

GLASSWARE: Collins glass

GARNISH: Preserved fig, rosemary sprig

- 2¾ oz. | 82 ml Figenza Mediterranean Fig Flavored Vodka
- ¾ oz. | 22.5 ml fresh lemon juice
- ½ oz. | 15 ml Vanilla Reàl
- Citrus tonic, to top

1. Combine all of the ingredients, except for the citrus tonic, in a cocktail shaker with ice and shake up vigorously.
2. Strain the cocktail into a collins glass and top off with the citrus tonic.
3. Garnish with the preserved fig and rosemary.

TUCSON SOUR

TESOTA
300 WEST CAMELBACK ROAD, PHOENIX

The base of this very attractive cocktail uses Sentinel from Whiskey Del Bac, a Tucson distillery. Although Whiskey Del Bac produces most of its collection in Tucson, Sentinel is a blend of Indiana whiskies that are finished off in Whiskey Del Bac casks and filtered over Mesquite charcoal with a touch of heat from the Sonoran desert.

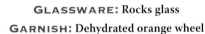

GLASSWARE: Rocks glass

GARNISH: Dehydrated orange wheel

- 2 oz. | 60 ml Sentinel Straight Rye Whiskey
- ½ oz. | 15 ml orgeat
- ½ oz. | 15 ml dry curaçao
- ½ oz. | 15 ml fresh lemon juice
- Red wine, to float

1. Combine all of the ingredients, except for the red wine, in a shaker tin with ice and shake vigorously.
2. Strain the cocktail into a rocks glass.
3. Top with a red wine float and garnish with a dehydrated orange wheel.

WHITE TAI

TESOTA
300 WEST CAMELBACK ROAD, PHOENIX

In Uptown, Tesota has settled in along Camelback Road, offering an international menu and an equally diverse cocktail list. Its rum-based White Tai reflects the approachable atmosphere of the restaurant and bar.

GLASSWARE: Highball glass
GARNISH: Mint, fresh orchid

- 1½ oz. | 45 ml white rum
- ¾ oz. | 22.5 ml fresh lime juice
- ¾ oz. | 22.5 ml passion fruit liqueur
- ½ oz. | 15 ml orgeat

1. Combine all of the ingredients in a shaker tin with ice and shake vigorously.
2. Strain the cocktail into a highball then add crushed ice.
3. Garnish with mint and a fresh orchid.

WHERE THERE'S SMOKE

Sat atop the roof of Rise Uptown Phoenix is retro cocktail bar Don Woods' Say When. With a 1970s theme, cozy interior, and jaw-dropping skyline views, it's a great spot for visitors and locals alike. Where the bar team works to resurrect cocktails forgotten by time, the menu is filled with throwbacks.

‖

GLASSWARE: Nick & Nora glass
GARNISH: Lime wheel cut in half and dipped in Tajín

- ¾ oz. | 22.5 ml Del Maguey Vida Clásico
- ¾ oz. | 22.5 ml Aperol
- ¾ oz. | 22.5 ml maraschino liqueur
- ¾ oz. | 22.5 ml fresh lime juice
- 7 to 8 drops habanero tincture

1. Freeze a Nick & Nora glass. Combine all of the ingredients in a cocktail shaker with ice and vigorously shake everything up.
2. Double-strain the cocktail into the frozen Nick & Nora.
3. Garnish with a Tajín-dusted lime.

SONORAN KATANA

Named after Don Woods, a prominent real estate agent in the 1950s, the cocktail bar now occupies the same building where his Phoenix office was situated. In the Rise Uptown Hotel, take the stairs or elevator in the middle of the building to get up to the rooftop bar. The brightness of the Sonoran Katana is almost as mesmerizing as the excellent Camelback Mountain scene visible from there.

||

GLASSWARE: Pilsner glass
GARNISH: Cucumber coins cut on a bias, purple orchid

- 2 cucumber coins
- 1 thick slice jalapeño
- ¼ oz. | 7.5 ml Stirrings Simple Syrup
- ¾ oz. | 22.5 ml fresh lime juice
- ¾ oz. | 22.5 ml Midori
- 1¼ oz. | 45 ml blanco tequila
- Soda water, to top

1. Freeze a pilsner glass. Muddle the jalapeño and cucumber coins in a shaker tin.
2. Add the remaining ingredients, except for the soda, along with ice and shake approximately 7 to 8 times to not overdilute the drink.
3. Strain the cocktail over ice into the frozen pilsner glass and top with supercharged soda water.
4. Garnish with two cucumber coins and a purple orchid.

HIDDEN ISLAND

LYLO SWIM CLUB
400 WEST CAMELBACK ROAD, PHOENIX

Pool life is extremely important for Valley residents who are left to sweat it out through the summer. During the slower season, resorts and hotels open up their pools to locals, offering day passes alongside DJs, seasonal bites, and fun summery cocktails. Lylo Swim Club is a popular option in Phoenix's Uptown neighborhood, with mid-century modern vibes and a poolside bar.

GLASSWARE: Catalina or pilsner glass

GARNISH: Grapefruit slices, mint

- 1½ oz. | 45 ml vanilla vodka
- 1 oz. | 30 ml fresh lime juice
- 1 oz. | 30 ml Simple Syrup (see recipe on page 20)
- ½ oz. | 15 ml Giffard Crème de Pamplemousse Rose
- ½ oz. | 15 ml Giffard Crème de Pêche

1. Get all of those ingredients into a cocktail shaker and add ice.
2. Shake for 10 seconds.
3. Strain the cocktail into a catalina or pilsner glass filled with crushed ice.
4. Using tweezer tongs, place the grapefruit slices in the glass between the ice and the inner glass wall.
5. Garnish with mint and any fun flamingo figurines you have laying around.

ARCADIA AND
BILTMORE

ORIGINAL TEQUILA SUNRISE

THE PHOENIX

PRIDE

LUST

ARCADIA ORANGE CRUSH

LITTLE LI SHOU

THE CRADLE & KEY

NOBODY WANTS ME

The Arcadia and Biltmore neighborhoods of Phoenix are important to the history of the city, having achieved their status when citrus farmers occupied the area near the Arizona Canal. The Biltmore district is relatively small, encompassing the region right around the Arizona Biltmore resort. To the east is Arcadia, an eye-catching section that bleeds into Scottsdale and is chock-full of adorable shops, upscale dining, and desirable older homes with lush landscaping.

Opened in 1929, the Arizona Biltmore was heavily influenced by Frank Lloyd Wright's designs, although Wright himself was not officially involved in the project. A treasured piece of art deco architecture full of stained glass, manicured lawns, and a regal atmosphere, the resort was conceived as a way to help boost the relatively new state as a tourist destination. It boasts the world's second-largest gold leaf ceiling. It's where the socialites of yesteryear came to see and be seen; just as importantly, it's where the infamous Tequila Sunrise was born.

ORIGINAL TEQUILA SUNRISE

ARIZONA BILTMORE
2400 EAST MISSOURI AVENUE, PHOENIX

First created at the Arizona Biltmore by Gene Sulit, the Original Tequila Sunrise is still proudly served today at the resort, where oversized chess games and art deco architecture create a stunning sipping environment.

||||

GLASSWARE: Este Tumbler pint glass
GARNISH: Blood orange wheel

- ¾ oz. | 22.5 ml fresh lime juice
- ¾ oz. | 22.5 ml Lejay Cassis
- ¼ oz. | 7.5 ml grenadine
- 2 oz. | 60 ml Don Julio Blanco Tequila

1. Build the ingredients up in the order listed in a beer glass.
2. Top with crushed ice.
3. Garnish with a blood orange wheel.

THE PHOENIX

SANTO ARCADIA
4418 EAST OSBORN ROAD, PHOENIX

The Phoenix was crowned the official cocktail of Phoenix in 2024 by the city's mayor, in collaboration with Milagro tequila. "Our very own Nicole Long beat out all the competition from rival bars and restaurants in town, securing her place in Phoenix cocktail history," says Adrian Galindo.

||||

GLASSWARE: Coupe glass
GARNISH: Dehydrated lemon slice

- **2 oz. | 60 ml reposado tequila**
- **1 oz. | 30 ml fresh lemon juice**
- **1 oz. | 30 ml Hot Honey Syrup (see recipe)**
- **¼ oz. | 7.5 ml Prickly Reàl**

1. Combine all of the ingredients in a shaker tin with ice and shake it up until cold.
2. Double-strain the cocktail into a coupe.
3. Garnish with a dehydrated lemon slice.

HOT HONEY SYRUP: Make a Honey Syrup (see recipe on page 20) and add chiltepin, to taste. After steeping, strain.

ADRIAN GALINDO, PECADO ARCADIA

What's your favorite cocktail to make?

At home, I like straight mezcal (not a cocktail, I know), but at work, our Pride cocktail.

How did you get interested in cocktails and mixology?

After becoming more involved with some of the best restaurants in Phoenix, I came to appreciate cuisine more thoroughly. The flavors, ingredients, and culture surrounding food helped me to realize the importance and romanticism of a good meal or a good cocktail. Food and beverage is one of the keystone cultural exports that can connect anyone more deeply to their own and other cultures, but I think my favorite part about cocktails is that, at the end of the day, they don't really matter. Food at least gives us sustenance—it is a necessary consumable—but alcohol is just something we all drink to feel silly. I've always thought that even though you should take an immense amount of pride in your work, you also shouldn't take yourself too seriously, especially in what we do.

What do you find unique about Arizona's cocktail culture?

Phoenix feels like an underrecognized younger sibling; we don't get a chance on the national or international stages in the same way that LA, Chicago, or New York do. Not to say we don't get chances, but I definitely don't hear people talk the same way about cocktail bars in Phoenix even though there are some amazing ones. I think right now especially, everyone is balancing the hunger to perform at a high level with a pretty minimal ego.

What are some underrated ingredients you love to use and why?

Piloncillo, amari, and agave or sotol distillates. Piloncillo is a Mexican cane sugar that has a deep molasses flavor similar to demerara. Amaro is one of my favorite designations for the variety of available flavor and usual bitterness. Agave and sotol distillates are probably my favorite spirits to work with and, in my experience, heavily undervalued; they can be very similar to wines in the beautiful expression of appellation and terroir.

What's one thing about Arizona that you think people don't understand or is misconstrued?

I think one of the most misunderstood facets of Arizona is the culture. I have fielded a fair number of questions from people who have the understanding that Arizona is either all desert or just universities with no real metropolitan areas or identity of its own. Phoenix alone has seen immense growth with a focus on unique food, art, and music scenes. I do also really enjoy the fact that a lot of the people in Phoenix are transplants, because it means everyone brings their own touch in expanding the vibe of Phoenix and AZ in general.

PRIDE

PECADO ARCADIA
4418 EAST OSBORN ROAD, PHOENIX

This is one of bartender Adrian Galindo's favorite cocktails to make, and it's easy to see why.

GLASSWARE: Skull mug
GARNISH: Mint sprig, edible orchid, flaming dehydrated orange slice

- 2 oz. | 60 ml fresh pineapple juice
- 1 oz. | 30 ml fresh lime juice
- 1 oz. | 30 ml Banhez Mezcal
- 1 oz. | 30 ml Uruapan Charanda Blanco Rum
- ½ oz. | 15 ml John D. Taylor's Velvet Falernum
- ½ oz. | 15 ml L'Original Combier
- ½ oz. | 15 ml coconut syrup
- ½ oz. | 15 ml Hibiscus Pecan Orgeat (see recipe)
- 2 dashes Australian Bitters Company Aromatic Bitters
- 1 sleeve Bittermens 'Elemakule Tiki Bitters

1. Combine all of the ingredients in a cocktail shaker with ice and shake.
2. Strain the cocktail into a skull mug.
3. Add ice to top, then place the mint and orchid in the mug.
4. Spray the dehydrated orange slice with high-proof alcohol and light it on fire. For a little theatrics, dust the flame with powdered cinnamon.

HIBISCUS PECAN ORGEAT: Add 2 cups toasted unsalted pecans to a food processor and grind. In a saucepan over medium-low heat, combine 4½ oz. sugar and 4½ oz. water and bring the mixture to a simmer. Stir in the pecans and simmer for 5 minutes. Remove from heat, stir in 2 tablespoons dried hibiscus, and allow the orgeat to cool overnight. Strain through a cheesecloth.

LUST

PECADO ARCADIA
4418 EAST OSBORN ROAD, PHOENIX

Bartender Zion Monroe's Lust cocktail is usually adorned with a print of a beautiful woman, but even without the portrait, the drink decidedly invokes a sexy perfume. *Pecado* means "sin" in Spanish, and the speakeasy in the trendy Arcadia neighborhood leans into that theme with its 7 Deadly Sins menu. It's a natural contrast to the property's Santo ("saint") restaurant. For the egg white, you can substitute 1 barspoon powdered egg whites.

GLASSWARE: Coupe glass

GARNISH: Edible paper print (preferably of someone easy on the eyes)

- 1 oz. | 30 ml Gracias a Dios Agave Gin
- 1 oz. | 30 ml fresh lime juice
- ½ oz. | 15 ml elderflower liqueur
- ½ oz. | 15 ml Giffard Lichi-Li
- ½ oz. | 15 ml rose syrup
- ¼ oz. | 7.5 ml agave nectar
- 1 egg white
- Sparkling white wine, to top

1. Combine all of the ingredients, except for the egg whites and sparkling wine, in a cocktail shaker with ice and shake until cold.
2. Strain the mixture into a separate shaker (or reuse the same one but remove the ice) and add egg whites for a dry shake.
3. Shake again until frothy then double-strain the cocktail into a coupe.
4. Top with the sparkling white wine and garnish with the edible paper print.

ARCADIA ORANGE CRUSH

What's better than a great cocktail? A great cocktail that comes with a great cause! Opening in 2024, Pizza To The Rescue sits near Arcadia and down the street from the Arizona Biltmore. Dedicated to helping pups in need, the bar teamed up with a local shelter, the Almost There Rescue, to donate a hefty percentage from all pizza sales to the shelter. It doesn't hurt that the drinks are on point, like this creamy, citrusy concoction.

GLASSWARE: Collins glass
GARNISH: Dehydrated orange slice

- 1½ oz. | 45 ml Espolón Tequila Blanco
- ½ oz. | 15 ml cream of coconut
- ¼ oz. | 7.5 ml Simple Syrup (see recipe on page 20)
- ¼ oz. | 7.5 ml fresh lime juice
- 1 oz. | 30 ml fresh mandarin juice
- ½ oz. | 15 ml Alma Finca Orange Liqueur

1. Combine all of the ingredients in a cocktail shaker with ice and shake until well chilled.
2. Double-strain the cocktail into a collins glass over fresh ice.
3. Garnish by blowtorching the edge of a dehydrated orange slice and placing the slice on top of the drink.

JASON ASHER, CENTURY GRAND

What's your favorite cocktail to make?

The Margarita.

How did you get interested in cocktails and mixology?

Central to my love for bartending is a strong appreciation for the connections I make with others. I am captivated by the different stories each person brings to the bar, and I am always drawn to the art of storytelling. As I hear the tales revealed through conversation, I am motivated to infuse the emotions, experiences, and personalities into the drinks I create.

Bartending has provided me with a special avenue to blend my fondness for socializing with my creative nature. Every cocktail I mix serves as a canvas on which I can depict the story behind the drink. By incorporating these narratives into my concoctions, I am able to provide customers not just with a drink, but with a personally tailored experience that touches their hearts.

As I refine my bartending abilities, I am always on the lookout for new stories to incorporate into my repertoire, eager to delve deeper into the lives of those who sit at my bar. Bartending has evolved into more than just a profession for me; it is a platform through which I can celebrate the richness of human diversity and pay tribute to the individual narratives that render each person truly extraordinary.

What influences you as a mixologist?

My creative process is fueled by history, geography, and the unique ingredients I am fortunate to have access to. These elements blend together to form the foundation of my culinary creations, enabling me to tell stories through my cocktails that resonate with our guests. By drawing inspiration from a myriad of sources, I am able to craft menus that not only satiate the palate but also spark a sense of wonder and curiosity, inviting drinkers on a sensory journey that transcends mere sustenance and delves into the realm of artistry and storytelling.

What do you find unique about Arizona's cocktail culture?

The Arizona cocktail community has experienced tremendous growth and evolution in recent years as bartenders, mixologists, and cocktail enthusiasts have banded together to create a united front. The synergy and camaraderie within the Arizona cocktail community have fostered a supportive environment for talented individuals to showcase their craft, experiment with new ideas, and push the boundaries of mixology. Through events, workshops, and collaborations, these passionate individuals have been able to exchange knowledge, share techniques, and inspire one another to continuously innovate and refine their craft.

What are some underrated ingredients you love to use and why?

Exploring the world of flavors is a passion of mine, especially when it involves uncovering new and unique ingredients. One such discovery that has captivated me is osmanthus, a flowering plant native to Japan known for its enchanting aroma and delectable taste. Often referred to as the "love blossom," osmanthus blooms in autumn, releasing a fragrance that evokes images of ripe peaches.

The ability of osmanthus to mimic the flavor of peach is fascinating, as it offers a fresh and delightful twist to traditional cocktail creations. Incorporating this exotic ingredient into cocktails adds a layer of complexity and intrigue, enticing the senses with its alluring aroma and sweet, fruity taste.

What's an accomplishment or point of pride in your career?

Receiving the coveted title of Best U.S. Cocktail Bar at Tales of the Cocktail Foundation Spirited Awards last year was undeniably a career highlight for me and the rest of our incredible team. It not only recognizes our dedication and passion for the craft of mixology but also re-affirms the countless hours of hard work and determination we have poured into creating exceptional experiences for our patrons. I am grateful for the opportunity to showcase our talents on such a prestigious platform, and I am incredibly proud of all that we have accomplished together.

CENTURY GRAND

It's hard enough to create a concept strong enough to drive a creative cocktail bar, but to come up with three distinct concepts sharing one location is a different task. Mixologist extraordinaire and co-owner Jason Asher was up for it, however, and has pulled it off spectacularly. Century Grand, a nondescript building that gives no hint as to the glamour inside, was named Best U.S. Cocktail Bar at Tales of the Cocktail Foundation Spirited Awards in 2023.

Upon entering the building, the lighting is dim, and to the right is the entrance of UnderTow, an immersive clipper ship experience that takes you down into the belly of an old wooden ship, while to the left is a waiting area between the other two bars, Platform 18 and Grey Hen Rx.

Step inside Platform 18, and it's a 1924 Presidential Pullman train car. A few steps across and suddenly you're in Grey Hen Rx's 19th century New Orleans apothecary. Overall, the details are exquisite—sights, sounds, and physical materials envelop you and transport you to times long gone.

LITTLE LI SHOU

THE GREY HEN RX
3626 EAST INDIAN SCHOOL ROAD, PHOENIX

A guest favorite, to be certain," says Alex Downing, bar manager at The Grey Hen Rx. "Thai basil with kaffir lime is always a delight. When you add a touch of phó spice and bright lime and pineapple, this cocktail really delivers." The name is from Chinese mythology; Li Shou is the cat goddess left in charge of our world. In The Grey Hen Rx's immersive narrative experience, the heroine, Emilie Grey, has named her own Siamese cat Li Shou.

GLASSWARE: Footed pint glass

GARNISH: Bamboo leaf, bamboo straw, orchid, toasted coconut flake

- 2 dashes Phó Spice Tincture (see recipe)
- ¼ oz. | 7.5 ml Kaffir Lime Cordial (see recipe)
- ¼ oz. | 7.5 ml Coco López Cream of Coconut
- 1 oz. | 30 ml pineapple juice
- ½ oz. | 15 ml fresh lime juice
- ¼ oz. | 7.5 ml Giffard Crème de Pêche
- ½ oz. | 15 ml Heirloom Genepy Liqueur
- 2 oz. | 60 ml Thai Basil–Infused Absolut Elyx (see recipe)

1. Prepare your glassware by wrapping a bamboo leaf around the glass until it's exposed over the lip of the glass.

2. Build your cocktail in a clean shaker tin, measuring out each ingredient carefully, in the order listed, and shake vigorously with ice.

3. Strain the cocktail over new ice into your footed pint glass and finish with crushed ice to fill.

4. Add your bamboo straw and orchid, then lightly sprinkle on a pinch of toasted coconut flake.

PHÓ SPICE TINCTURE: Using a tea infuser basket, steep phó spice blend in 8 oz. overproof vodka overnight. Remove or strain the spices out and add the tincture to an eye dropper.

KAFFIR LIME CORDIAL: In a saucepan over medium-high heat, combine 1 cup sugar, 1 cup water, and 4 kaffir lime leaves, sliced into strips, and bring the mixture to a boil, stirring until the sugar is dissolved. Reduce the heat and simmer for about 8 minutes, until the syrup smells of lime leaves. Add 2 oz. fresh lime juice and simmer gently until the liquid thickens. Remove the cordial from heat and let it cool. Strain, cover, and refrigerate.

THAI BASIL–INFUSED ABSOLUT ELYX: In a bowl, gently muddle a handful of Thai basil leaves. Add the muddled leaves to 1 (750 ml) bottle of Absolut Elyx Vodka and allow the infusion to sit for at least 4 hours. Strain and rebottle.

THE CRADLE & KEY

UNDERTOW
3626 EAST INDIAN SCHOOL ROAD, PHOENIX

"The amazing thing about Jason Asher's palate," says his partner and vice president of operations, Mat Snapp, "is that he's already planned for how the cocktail will evolve as you enjoy it. This cocktail has four house infusions in it, and every layer is noticeable individually and in unison. It's some kind of wizardry, I think."

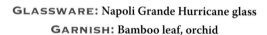

GLASSWARE: Napoli Grande Hurricane glass
GARNISH: Bamboo leaf, orchid

- 1 oz. | 30 ml Toasted Coconut Infused–Rum (see recipe)
- ½ oz. | 15 ml Banks 5 Island Blend Rum
- ½ oz. | 15 ml Annatto-Infused Mezcal (see recipe)
- ¼ oz. | 7.5 ml Dandelion Root–Infused Passion Fruit Liqueur (see recipe)
- ¼ oz. | 7.5 ml Strawberry-Infused Gentian Liqueur (see recipe)
- ½ oz. | 15 ml Kalani Coconut Liqueur
- ½ oz. | 15 ml Guava Reàl
- 1 oz. | 30 ml fresh lime juice
- 1 oz. | 30 ml pineapple juice
- ¼ oz. | 7.5 ml Simple Syrup (see recipe on page 20)
- 2 dashes elixir of life mushroom extract tincture
- 2 dashes 10% Saline Solution (see recipe on page 20)

1. In a clean shaker tin or mixing glass, measure and add each of your ingredients carefully, in the order listed.
2. Add 1½ cups crushed ice and blend using a spindle blender.
3. Slowly pour the cocktail from the blending tin into a hurricane glass and top with crushed ice.
4. Garnish with a bamboo leaf and an orchid.

DANDELION ROOT–INFUSED PASSION FRUIT LIQUEUR: In a large sealable jar, combine 1 cup Giffard Crème de Fruits de la Passion with 1 to 2 tablespoons dried dandelion root or roasted dandelion root tea and seal the jar. Shake, allow the infusion to sit for at least 2 hours, and strain.

TOASTED COCONUT INFUSED–RUM: In a large sealable jar, combine 1 cup Wray & Nephew White Overproof Rum and 1 to 2 tablespoons unsweetened toasted coconut flakes, seal the jar, and shake. Let the infusion sit for 2 to 24 hours and strain.

ANNATTO-INFUSED MEZCAL: In a large sealable jar, combine 1 cup 400 Conejos Espadín — Tobalá and 1 to 2 teaspoons whole annatto seeds, seal the jar, and shake. Let the infusion sit for 4 to 24 hours and strain.

STRAWBERRY-INFUSED GENTIAN LIQUEUR: In a glass container, gently muddle a handful of ripe strawberries. Add 1 (750 ml) bottle of Suze L'Originale, seal the jar, and shake. Allow the infusion to sit for 4 to 12 hours and fine-strain.

NIKKI LONG, BACANORA MANAGEMENT GROUP

Nicole (Nikki) Long was named a Top 10 finalist for U.S. Bartender of the Year category in the 2024 Tales of the Cocktail Foundation Spirited Awards.

What's your cocktail to make?

My favorite cocktail to make is a Smoke Bitters Pineapple Mezcal Sour with egg white. I love how the smokiness of the mezcal pairs with the tropical sweetness of pineapple, creating a rich and complex flavor. The smoke bitters add a unique depth, while the egg white gives the cocktail a silky texture and a frothy finish. It's a drink that's both visually striking and incredibly satisfying to make.

How did you get interested in cocktails and mixology?

I began my journey in dive bars while pursuing a degree in agriculture, but after the pandemic hit, I shifted my focus to cocktails. I joined Social Hall in Tempe, where I had the privilege of learning from the incredible owner, Michael Kenney. Under his mentorship, I grew from a brunch bartender to the bar manager over four years. When Michael sold the bar in 2023, I seized the opportunity to dive into a new challenge at Santo/Pecado.

What influences you as a mixologist?

The diverse cultures within my blended family. Living in Arizona also gives me access to native plants like prickly pear, mesquite, agave, and cholla buds, which I draw inspiration from, incorporating these desert flavors into my creations. I'm passionate about using ingredients I've grown in my own garden, adding a personal touch that reflects a piece of me in every drink. Whenever possible, I source locally grown ingredients, following a farm-to-cocktail approach. This makes each drink special, using sustainably grown produce that's only available at peak freshness during specific times of the year. For me, cocktails are more than just a drink—they celebrate both the spirit and the growing season, making every creation a one-of-a-kind, limited-edition experience.

What do you find unique about Arizona's cocktail culture?

The remarkable support within Arizona's bartending community. It's a close-knit network where we not only help each other on a personal level but also collaborate as businesses. I've been fortunate to learn from incredible mentors like Adrian Galindo, my current beverage director. Their guidance and welcoming environment of the local bartending scene have allowed me to grow and push the boundaries of my craft. This spirit of camaraderie is a cornerstone of Arizona's cocktail culture and something I deeply value.

What are some underrated ingredients you love to use and why?

One of my favorites is the chiltepin pepper. While jalapeños are more commonly used, chiltepin peppers offer a distinct smoky heat that brings a unique depth to cocktails. Their small size is no indicator of their bold flavor, providing a spiciness that enhances rather than dominates. It's also Arizona's only native pepper, so it's natural to incorporate them into my drinks.

What's an accomplishment or point of pride in your career?

The honor of creating the official cocktail of Phoenix. This achievement, combined with integration of locally sourced and homegrown ingredients into my cocktails, is a major accomplishment.

NOBODY WANTS ME

Helen Morgan was an infamous Broadway performer and lounge singer in New York in the 1920s. She would sing a "torchy" (a sad love song) called "Nobody Wants Me," often performing from atop the piano in the orchestra pit or at nearby club, Chez Morgan. "Contrary to its name, this cocktail is the most popular drink on the menu for good reason," says Nicole (Nikki) Long, bar manager of Platform 18, and a finalist for the 2024 U.S. Bartender of the Year category in the Tales of the Cocktail Foundation Spirited Awards. "First, it's perfectly balanced—not too sweet and very refreshing. Plus, it's beautiful! You can't help but feel like a queen with the glass it's served in!"

GLASSWARE: Bormioli Rocco 8½ oz. etched stem glass

- **Pink peppercorns, finely ground, for the rim**
- **1½ oz. | 45 ml Ana María Tequila Rosa**
- **½ oz. | 15 ml Mint-Infused Gin (see recipe)**
- **½ oz. | 15 ml pineapple juice**
- **½ oz. | 15 ml foaming clarified rhubarb syrup**
- **½ oz. | 15 ml fresh lime juice**
- **¼ oz. | 7.5 ml Giffard Crème de Pamplemousse Rose**
- **¼ oz. | 7.5 ml Giffard Crème de Pêche**
- **¼ oz. | 7.5 ml Sumac Berry Syrup (see recipe)**
- **Dash Pink Peppercorn Tincture (see recipe)**
- **Dash Fine Pink Peppercorn Dust (see recipe)**

1. Wet the rim of a stem glass then dip the glass into finely crushed pink peppercorn powder to give it a rim.

2. As this cocktail substitutes a foaming syrup for egg white, it requires a reverse dry shake. To do this, combine all of the ingredients in a cocktail shaker with ice and shake vigorously.

3. Strain the mixture into a second clean cocktail shaker tin (or pour it back into the same tin without ice) and shake. This will give your cocktail a luscious layer of aromatic foam when you slowly pour it into the glass.

MINT-INFUSED GIN: In a bowl, muddle a handful of mint leaves. Add the muddled leaves to 1 (750 ml) bottle of gin. Let the gin infuse for 24 hours before straining out the leaves.

SUMAC BERRY SYRUP: Make Simple Syrup (see recipe on page 20), adding 1 tablespoon sumac berries while simmering. Strain when the syrup is cool.

DASH PINK PEPPERCORN TINCTURE: Steep 5 oz. pink peppercorns in 8 oz. overproof vodka for 24 hours. Strain the tincture into an eye dropper.

SCOTTSDALE

IN THE MOOD FOR LOVE	GOLD CHAINS
ONE TIME THING	NEGRONI ISOLA
LAVENDER BEE'S KNEES	NO. 100
CRESCENT MOON OLD FASHIONED	SPA WATER
FIG & THYME OLD FASHIONED	ESPRESS YA' SELF
MEZ-CALA	ORANGE CARDAMOM ESPRESSO MARTINI
BARBARY FIG MARGARITA	YOU'RE WELCOME
"SMOKEY BEAR-IES"	IT'S GOLD!
MATSURI MEZCALITA	CHARTREUPHY
AIRPARK	TIME STANDS STILL SAGE'ARITA
GOLDEN YEARS	EL CADILLAC
VERSACE ON THE FLOOR	THE JALISCO OLD FASHIONED
IT'S NOT THAT DEEP	

Oh Scottsdale, your reputation precedes you. A little unfairly actually. Yes, there are the nightclubs, boisterous bars, and people with a lot of money running around, but Scottsdale is much more than just Old Town. The venues in this chapter run the gamut, including hotel and resort bars, which is fair considering Scottsdale is home to more than seventy resorts and hotels. Just like Las Vegas or LA, we've got some amazing places churning out craveable drinks, and it just so happens you can sleep above these locales, too.

That's because no matter how much the state has grown, has headed in more modern directions, or has been on trend, a few givens will always be part of the profile:

- There are a lot of snowbirds
- It's impossible to be a bored golfer
- Resorts are a part of everyday life

Storied resorts are flung across Scottsdale's one hundred and eighty-plus square miles. From Hotel Valley Ho and The Wigwam to upcoming locations like the W Scottsdale or The Global Ambassador, residents love these locations for providing some summer staycation relief, when properties drop rates during the slow tourist season. If you're a Phoenician riding out the heat, sometimes a weekend at a five-star place with a cheaper price and access to its pools is the only way to keep your sanity. Many hotels and resorts accept daily reservations just for the pool alone. Along with that comes DJs, creative food stations, and drinks. Lots and lots of drinks!

IN THE MOOD FOR LOVE

TELL YOUR FRIENDS
17797 NORTH SCOTTSDALE RD, SCOTTSDALE

An underground Prohibition-style speakeasy with vibes, Tell Your Friends is a small and intimate cocktail lounge with sizzling live music and not-your-standard drink menu. Case in point is the savory-leaning In the Mood for Love, in which bartender Keifer Gilbert pairs a simple red bell pepper syrup against clean gin flavor and a little bit of tart raspberry sweetness.

GLASSWARE: Collins glass

GARNISH: Mint, raspberries, dehydrated blood orange wheel

- 1½ oz. | 45 ml Tanqueray N° Ten Gin
- ¾ oz. | 22.5 ml Red Bell Pepper Syrup (see recipe)
- 3 raspberries
- ½ oz. | 15 ml Dolin Génépy le Chamois Liqueur
- Juice of 1 lime

1. In the bottom of a cocktail shaker, muddle 3 raspberries.
2. Combine the remaining ingredients in the tin, add ice, and shake well.
3. Strain the cocktail into a collins glass with fresh ice cubes.
4. Garnish with fresh mint, raspberries, and a dehydrated blood orange wheel.

RED BELL PEPPER SYRUP: Slice and de-seed 4 red bell peppers then run the pieces through a juicer. Fine-strain the juice, then measure, and combine the juice with an equal volume of sugar (1:1 juice to sugar). Stir until the sugar is dissolved.

ONE TIME THING

TELL YOUR FRIENDS
17797 NORTH SCOTTSDALE ROAD, SCOTTSDALE

Smooth and sippable, One Time Thing is highlighted by the contrast of the sweet, creamy banana flavor against the oaky cognac. It's even more enjoyable with a three-piece jazz band playing in the background on a sultry Saturday night in Scottsdale, when ordering this drink is unlikely to be a "one-time thing." However, it's just as good made at home with some jazz on the stereo!

GLASSWARE: Rocks glass
GARNISH: Banana chip

- 1½ oz. | 45 ml Rémy Martin 1738 Accord Royal
- ½ oz. | 15 ml Amaro Montenegro
- ½ oz. | 15 ml Giffard Banane du Brésil
- ½ oz. | 15 ml oloroso sherry
- ¼ oz. | 7.5 ml Banana Reàl
- Orange peel, to express

1. Combine all of the ingredients, except for the orange peel, in a Yarai mixing glass with ice and stir.
2. Strain the cocktail into a rocks glass with one large ice cube.
3. Express and discard an orange peel over the drink before carefully placing a banana chip in the drink.

LAVENDER BEE'S KNEES

PROOF
10600 EAST CRESCENT MOON DRIVE, SCOTTSDALE

Proof bartender Autumn West's cocktail riffs on the classic Bee's Knees with the addition of lavender, which is grown on farms around the state.

⫴

GLASSWARE: Coupe glass
GARNISH: Dehydrated lemon slice with a decorative bee

- Lavender Crystal Sugar (see recipe), for the rim
- 2 oz. | 60 ml Botanist gin
- ½ oz. | 15 ml St-Germain Elderflower Liqueur
- ¾ oz. | 22.5 ml fresh lemon juice
- ¾ oz. | 22.5 ml Lavender-Infused Honey (see recipe)

1. Dip the rim of a coupe glass in water, then dip it in Lavender Crystal Sugar to give the glass a rim.
2. Combine the remaining ingredients in a cocktail shaker with ice and shake vigorously.
3. Strain the cocktail into the coupe.
4. Garnish with a dehydrated lemon slice with a decorative bee.

LAVENDER CRYSTAL SUGAR: Combine 1 tablespoon culinary lavender with a 2 to 3 tablespoons of sugar in a coffee grinder. Blend until the lavender is finely ground. Dump the mixture into a bowl and whisk in additional sugar until the sugar amounts to 1 cup. Store in an airtight container.

LAVENDER-INFUSED HONEY: In a small saucepan over medium heat, combine 1½ oz. loose lavender flowers, 2 oz. hot water, and 8 oz. fresh Arizona honey and remove the pot from heat just before boiling. Allow the honey to cool to room temperature then fine-strain.

CRESCENT MOON OLD FASHIONED

PROOF
10600 EAST CRESCENT MOON DRIVE, SCOTTSDALE

I was born up north in Flagstaff," says Proof bartender Autumn West, "under a crescent moon. Now I get to create cocktails here on Crescent Moon Drive." Local Arizona blood orange lifts the fruit-forward flavor here, making it easy to drink at the signature bar for the Four Seasons Resort Scottsdale. "This is a well-balanced, cocktail," says West. "It has everything you look for in an Old Fashioned without floating, muddled fruit."

GLASSWARE: Crystal rocks glass
GARNISH: Slice of dehydrated blood orange, Luxardo maraschino cherry

- 2 oz. | 60 ml Angel's Envy Kentucky Straight Bourbon
- ½ oz. | 15 ml Luxardo Maraschino Originale
- ½ oz. | 15 ml blood orange puree
- 1 barspoon Demerara Simple Syrup (see recipe on page 20)
- 2 dashes Angostura bitters
- 2 dashes orange bitters

1. Combine all of the ingredients, except for the bitters, in a mixing glass.
2. Add the ice and bitters.
3. Stir 15 times.
4. Strain the cocktail over one large ice cube.
5. Garnish with a dehydrated blood orange slice and a Luxardo cherry.

FIG & THYME OLD FASHIONED

THE ITALIANO
9301 EAST SHEA BOULEVARD, #137, SCOTTSDALE

This is a more classic, wintery interpretation of an Old Fashioned. It is full of spice, warm fall flavors, and a robust bite—just the thing for when the mercury actually does drop. Winter months in Arizona run the gamut; world class skiing exists in the northern and eastern regions of the state, and even Phoenix dips into freezing territory at night. If you've never seen the Sedona red rocks dusted in snow or watched Glendale Glitters in the cold, have you really been to AZ?

GLASSWARE: Double rocks glass
GARNISH: Orange peel, thyme bundle, sliced dried fig

- 2 oz. | 60 ml Woodford Reserve Kentucky Straight Bourbon Whiskey
- ½ oz. | 15 ml Fig & Thyme Syrup (see recipe)

- 2 dashes Fee Brothers Cardamom Bitters
- 2 dashes Angostura bitters

1. In a Yarai mixing glass, combine all of the ingredients.
2. Add ice and stir 40 to 60 rotations.
3. Using a julep strainer, strain cocktail over a large square cube in a double rocks glass.
4. Peel and express an orange peel over the cocktail and add the peel as a garnish alongside a thyme bundle and sliced dried fig.

FIG & THYME SYRUP: Chop 1 cup figs, fresh or dried, and strip thyme leaves from 1 bunch fresh thyme. Bring 1 cup water to a boil. Whisk in 1 cup sugar, the fig pieces, and the thyme leaves, and simmer for 10 to 12 minutes. Remove the mixture from heat, allow it to cool completely, and strain.

MEZ-CALA

CALA

7501 EAST CAMELBACK ROAD, SCOTTSDALE

This one is definitely a tribute to the desert. Flavors like prickly pear and green chile remind you of where you are in the world, while blackberry and ginger poke through. It all plays off as a great counterpoint to CALA's coastal Mediterranean menu at the bottom of The Senna House in Scottsdale's renowned Old Town.

GLASSWARE: Coupe glass

GARNISH: Fresh blackberry and dehydrated lime wheel on a skewer

- 1 oz. | 30 ml 400 Conejos Espadín Joven Mezcal
- 1 oz. | 30 ml St. George Green Chile Vodka
- ½ oz. | 15 ml fresh lime juice
- ½ oz. | 15 ml blackberry liqueur
- ¾ oz. | 22.5 ml Liquid Alchemist Prickly Pear Cocktail Syrup
- ¼ oz. | 7.5 ml ginger syrup
- ¼ oz. | 7.5 ml aquafaba

1. Combine all of the ingredients in a cocktail shaker then fill the tin halfway with ice.
2. Shake for 15 seconds.
3. Strain the cocktail into a coupe.
4. Garnish with a fresh blackberry skewered on top of a deyhdrated lime wheel.

CHRISTINE LORD AND BERKELEY ALVARADO, TEQUILA GODDESSES

How did you get interested in agave spirits?

Christine: As a bartender, I always liked tequila. In 2015, when I moved to Arizona from Buffalo, New York, I was exposed to so many additional tequilas and mezcals, and my curiosity grew from there.

Berkeley: I started my career as a tequila goddess in 2021. It was something I was hesitant about because I knew there were so many things to learn about all of the agave spirit varieties. But since then, I've studied, taken numerous trips to Tequila, and I am now Consejo Regulador de Tequila (CRT)-certified and can speak to the two hundred–plus selections we have here at La Hacienda.

What influences you as a tequila goddess?

Christine: I am always looking for new agave spirits, and I focus on the way they are made and the people making them.

Berkeley: There are so many stories behind different tequilas. I enjoy learning about the history of who started the distillery, where the agave is grown, the family history, and the methods of how they do things differently. All of that knowledge is what drives me.

What do you find unique about Arizona's cocktail culture?

Christine: People are increasingly aware of what they are drinking and are now seeking out smaller producers and small-batch barrels that are additive-free.

What are some underrated ingredients you love to use and why?

Christine: Raicilla and bacanora, for sure. They're so unique and a great way to showcase other parts of Mexico.

Berkeley: Raicilla is something I believe is extremely underrated, and people just don't know much about it. It is a fun spirit; the flavors that come from it are very different.

What's an accomplishment or point of pride in your career?

Christine: I'm proud of everything I have come to know about agave spirits. I have taken and passed the CRT test twice and have had hands-on experience in Mexico to solidify my knowledge. Berkeley and I handpick a tequila barrel for La Hacienda, which is great to share with our guests.

Berkeley: A point in my career that I am most proud of is being recognized at AzTLA (Arizona Lodging and Tourism Association) for the hotel. Knowing that I worked my way into this position, studied hard, invested so much, and my time was being recognized was incredible.

Christine Lord

Berkeley Alvarado

BARBARY FIG MARGARITA

LA HACIENDA
7575 EAST PRINCESS DRIVE, SCOTTSDALE

This cocktail captures the essence of the region in a glass by using cacti fruit. The team at La Hacienda sources prickly pear fruit from the venue property to make their homemade syrup, and you can follow their recipe. You can also make your own hibiscus syrup, or buy it off the shelf from Monin or Torani.

GLASSWARE: Double rocks glass
GARNISH: Dehydrated lime wheel, edible flower

- 2 oz. | 60 ml blanco tequila
- 1 oz. | 30 ml fresh lime juice.
- ½ oz. | 15 ml Prickly Pear Cactus Syrup (see recipe)
- ¼ oz. | 7.5 ml hibiscus syrup

1. Combine all of the ingredients in a cocktail shaker with ice and shake for 15 to 20 seconds.
2. Place a large ice cube into a double rocks glass.
3. Double-strain the cocktail into the glass.
4. Garnish with dehydrated lime wheel and edible flower.

PRICKLY PEAR CACTUS SYRUP: Carefully pluck the fruit from the cactus, then, with a kitchen torch or grill flame, torch the fruit to remove the thorns while heating the fruit. In a blender, combine the fruit and sugar using a 2:1 ratio of fruit to sugar. Blend and strain.

"SMOKEY BEAR-IES"

THE PLAZA BAR
7575 EAST PRINCESS DRIVE, SCOTTSDALE

Bartenders Jose Garcia and John Wilhelm feature this on their summer menu at The Plaza Bar, as drinks are updated to reflect seasonal offerings. "This is a symphony of berries, passion fruit, vanilla, and the subtly spicy notes of the Oaxacan chile liqueur," they say. This pairs well with the bar's outdoor seating on hot summer nights, when the misters are at full tilt and you can't bear sitting inside anymore.

GLASSWARE: Double rocks glass
GARNISH: 3 raspberries on a pick

- 1½ oz. | 45 ml Hibiscus-Infused Mezcal (see recipe)
- ¾ oz. | 22.5 ml fresh lime juice
- ½ oz. | 15 ml Alma Tepec Licor de Chile Pasilla Mixe
- ½ oz. | 15 ml raspberry syrup
- ½ oz. | 15 ml Giffard Crème de Fraise des Bois
- ¼ oz. | 7.5 ml Liquid Alchemist Passion Fruit Cocktail Syrup
- 1 barspoon vanilla syrup

1. Combine all of the ingredients in a cocktail shaker with ice and shake for 15 to 20 seconds.
2. Place one large ice cube into the double rocks glass.
3. Double-strain the cocktail into the glass.
4. Garnish by skewering 3 raspberries on an adorable bear pick, if possible, then placing the pick on top of the glass.

HIBISCUS-INFUSED MEZCAL: Add 20 grams hibiscus tea flowers to 1 (750 ml) bottle of Mezcal NARAN. Let the infusion sit for 2 hours, double-strain, and rebottle.

MATSURI MEZCALITA

TORO LATIN RESTAURANT & RUM BAR
17020 HAYDEN ROAD, SCOTTSDALE

For any golf enthusiast, Toro is a solid option after a round at TPC Scottsdale or for delicious pan-Latin food with views of the championship eighteenth hole and McDowell Mountains. It carries one of the Valley's largest collection of rums, with over one hundred and fifty different varieties, and also has one of the biggest patios available for the area. The non-rum cocktails can still hold their own. This one carries a touch of Tajín, a favorite seasoning in this area of the country, in addition to the French ginger liqueur and Mexican corn liqueur.

GLASSWARE: Double rocks glass
GARNISH: Lime wheel dipped in Tajín

- 1½ oz. | 45 ml mezcal
- ¾ oz. | 22.5 ml Nixta Licor de Elote
- ¾ oz. | 22.5 ml fresh lime juice
- ¼ oz. | 7.5 ml Domaine de Canton
- ½ oz. | 15 ml Togarashi Syrup (see recipe)
- 2 dashes The Japanese Bitters Umami Bitters

1. Combine all of the ingredients in a cocktail shaker with ice and shake for approximately 20 seconds.
2. Double-strain the cocktail into a double rocks glass over one large ice cube.
3. Garnish with a lime wheel that's been dipped in Tajín.

TOGARASHI SYRUP: Make a thick (2:1) simple syrup (see recipe on page 20). Add 2 tablespoons togarashi to the syrup and allow the syrup to infuse. Strain and bottle.

AIRPARK

This cocktail, a variation of the Paper Plane, was named after the Scottsdale Airpark that sits near the Fairmont Scottsdale Princess resort. The Fairmont Scottsdale Princess receives their own barrel of bourbon from Maker's Mark that is blended just for them and used as the base of this drink. Keeping things local, Steadfast Farm from the city of Mesa provides the honey that balances things up.

GLASSWARE: Rocks glass

GARNISH: Orange peel, charred

- ¾ oz. | 22.5 ml Maker's Mark
- ¾ oz. | 22.5 ml Amaro Nonino Quintessentia
- ½ oz. | 15 ml Mesquite-Charred Lemon Juice (see recipe)

- ¾ oz. | 22.5 ml Aperol
- ½ oz. | 15 ml Honey Syrup (see recipe)
- 2 to 3 dashes Regans' Orange Bitters No. 6

1. Combine all of the ingredients in a cocktail shaker with ice and shake well for 10 to 15 seconds.
2. Add fresh ice to a rocks glass.
3. Double-strain the cocktail into the glass.
4. Express the orange peel over the drink then, using a cigar torch, char the peel and place it on top of the drink as a garnish. A little smoke should be wafting up.

MESQUITE-CHARRED LEMON JUICE: Halve 1 lemon and char it on a mesquite wood grill. Let the halves rest, then juice them and strain the through a fine-mesh strainer.

HONEY SYRUP: Thin out Steadfast Farms honey with equal parts hot water and let it rest.

GOLDEN YEARS

FAT OX
6316 NORTH SCOTTSDALE ROAD, SCOTTSDALE

This cocktail from Matt Carter's modern Italian restaurant includes Suze L'Originale, a bright yellow French aperitif dating to the late nineteenth century whose bittersweet taste comes courtesy of the wild gentian roots from the Alps. Suze's citrusy and herbal notes complement Fat Ox's in-house shrub made from peaches, lemongrass, and mint. A great fit for post-work happy hour.

GLASSWARE: Coupe glass

GARNISH: Dehydrated Candied Lemon with Marigold Petals
(see recipe)

- 1½ oz. | 45 ml Commerce Gin
- ¾ oz. | 22.5 ml White Peach, Lemongrass & Mint Shrub (see recipe)
- ½ oz. | 15 ml fresh lemon juice
- ½ oz. | 15 ml Suze L'Originale
- 2 oz. | 60 ml Vietti Moscato d'Asti, to top

1. Combine all of the ingredients, except for the Moscato, in a cocktail shaker with ice and shake.
2. Strain the cocktail into a coupe.
3. Top with the moscato and garnish with candied flower lemon.

WHITE PEACH, LEMONGRASS & MINT SHRUB: In a nonreactive container, combine 600 grams pitted white peaches and 600 grams white sugar. Let the sugar and peaches macerate overnight, then blend until smooth. Strain the mixture through a fine-mesh strainer. Add 600 ml lemongrass mint white balsamic vinegar, and store the shrub in the refrigerator.

DEHYDRATED CANDIED LEMON WITH MARIGOLD PETALS: Slice up 2 lemons and remove the seeds. Make Simple Syrup (see recipe on page 20), adding the lemon slices in one layer when simmering. Take out the slices when they are translucent, about 30 minutes, and place them on a cooling rack to dry for at least 12 hours. Add marigold petals on top when serving.

VERSACE ON THE FLOOR

THE AMERICANO
17797 NORTH SCOTTSDALE ROAD, SCOTTSDALE

The Versace on the Floor starts off with a cool and crisp, refreshing sweetness before moving into a spicy, peppery bite," says director of operations Kevin Ferguson. "Just when you think it's too much, the balsamic and olive oil foam kicks in to temper things with a savoriness." The unexpected flavors are a great way to spruce up a classic Martini.

GLASSWARE: Martini glass

GARNISH: Basil Olive Oil Foam (see recipe), basil leaf

- **2 oz. | 60 ml Serrano and Fresno Chile–Infused Vodka (see recipe)**
- **½ oz. | 15 ml Simple Syrup (see recipe on page 20)**
- **¾ oz. | 22.5 ml fresh lime juice**
- **¼ oz. | 7.5 ml Honey Syrup (see recipe)**
- **¼ oz. | 7.5 ml Saratoga Olive Oil Co. Coconut Balsamic Vinegar**

1. Combine all of the ingredients in a Boston shaker and shake well.

2. Strain the cocktail into a martini glass.

3. Top off with the Basil Olive Oil Foam and a basil leaf.

HONEY SYRUP: Thin out Crockett Mesquite Honey with equal parts hot water and let it rest.

SERRANO AND FRESNO CHILE–INFUSED VODKA: Add serrano and Fresno chile peppers, chopped, with or without seeds, to taste, to 1 (750 ml) bottle of vodka and infuse for at least 30 minutes. Strain and rebottle.

BASIL OLIVE OIL FOAM: In a saucepan over low heat, combine 1 cup basil-infused olive oil and 1 oz. mono-and-diglyceride flakes and stir until the flakes are dissolved. Allow the oil to cool, then add it to a whipping canister and charge with two charges. Cool and shake before use.

IT'S NOT THAT DEEP

THE AMERICANO
17797 NORTH SCOTTSDALE ROAD, SCOTTDALE

Originally opened by Scott Conant and now under the leadership of local celebrity chef Beau MacMillan, The Americano is a modern Italian-inspired steak house in the northern part of Scottsdale. Bartender Megan McFadden includes the spirit of the restaurant's strong wine list in this elegant floral cocktail.

GLASSWARE: Wineglass

GARNISH: Dried rose petals, lavender sprig

- Sugar, for the rim
- 1½ oz. | 45 ml Diega Ginebra Rosa
- ¾ oz. | 22.5 ml Monin Hibiscus Syrup
- ¾ oz. | 22.5 ml guava juice
- 1 oz. | 30 ml fresh lime juice
- Franciacorta, to top

1. Wet the rim of a wineglass then dip the rim into sugar to give it a rim. Combine the remaining ingredients, except for the franciacorta, into a cocktail shaker with ice and shake.

2. Strain the cocktail into the wineglass with fresh ice and top with franciacorta.

3. Garnish with dried rose petals and a lavender sprig.

GOLD CHAINS

THE ITALIANO
9301 EAST SHEA BOULEVARD #137, SCOTTSDALE

A spicy take on a Gold Rush with a little bit of mango flair, Gold Chains is representative of Arizona's Old West past with its heat, honey, and whiskey. "This cocktail really runs the gamut in terms of versatility," says mixologist Abby Kate Larson. "Some people think it tastes like it was designed to be crushed on a golf course or poolside, and some people can't put their finger on what it goes best with, but they know they'd like another one. It's just good fun."

GLASSWARE: Coupe glass
GARNISH: Thai chile pepper, gold dust

- 1½ oz. | 45 ml Four Roses Bourbon
- ¾ oz. | 22.5 ml Honey Syrup (see recipe on page 20)
- ¾ oz. | 22.5 ml red pepper puree
- ¾ oz. | 22.5 ml fresh lemon juice
- ¾ oz. | 22.5 ml Giffard Mango Liqueur
- ¾ oz. | 22.5 ml egg whites

1. Combine all of the ingredients in a cocktail shaker without ice and give it a vigorous dry shake to froth up the egg whites.
2. Add ice and shake again to dilute and chill.
3. Double-strain the cocktail into a coupe, ensuring debris from the pepper puree does not fall into the drink.
4. Garnish with gold dust, formed into a pattern with a barspoon, and then place a red Thai chile pepper to float.

NEGRONI ISOLA

I am always looking to do something funky and unique," says corporate mixologist Abby Kate Larson. "It doesn't have to be absurdly complicated in order to be crafted well. This drink walks that line between being a summer boating cocktail and a wintry fireside sipper." Larson adds that instead of using a coconut-infused rum, you could fat-wash the rum with coconut oil.

GLASSWARE: Double rocks glass

GARNISH: Orange twist

- Toasted coconut shavings, for the rim
- 1 oz. | 30 ml Planteray Cut & Dry Coconut Rum
- 1 oz. | 30 ml Cinnamon-Infused Campari (see recipe)
- 1 oz. | 30 ml Casals Mediterranean Vermouth

1. Combine all of the ingredients in a Yarai mixing glass.
2. Add ice and stir 40 to 60 rotations.
3. Rim a double rocks glass with toasted coconut shavings.
4. Strain the cocktail with a julep strainer into the glass with a large ice cube.
5. Peel and express an orange twist over the cocktail and then add the twist as a garnish.

CINNAMON-INFUSED CAMPARI: In a large mason jar, combine 1 (750 ml) bottle of Campari and 2 to 4 cinnamon sticks, to taste. Allow the mixture to infuse at room temperature for 5 days then strain and rebottle the Campari.

NO. 100

WINDSOR
5223 NORTH CENTRAL AVENUE, PHOENIX

Windsor's chill local-bar atmosphere fits in well with its namesake neighborhood. The historic area caters to those looking to hang out post-work and the rapidly growing young urbanite demographic that has moved into the Downtown and Uptown areas. Windsor's prohibition-style cocktails pair comfortably with their patio-friendly menu, like this No. 100 full of tropical and savory flavors.

GLASSWARE: Collins glass
GARNISH: Mint sprig

- 1 oz. | 30 ml white rum
- ½ oz. | 15 ml Caraway-Infused Mezcal (see recipe)
- ½ oz. | 15 ml Casa D'Aristi Huana Mayan Guanabana Liqueur
- ½ oz. | 15 ml fresh lemon juice
- ½ oz. | 15 ml peach syrup
- ½ oz. | 15 ml pineapple syrup
- ¼ oz. | 7.5 ml Dolin Blanc vermouth
- ¼ oz. | 7.5 ml The Bitter Truth Pimento Dram Allspice Liqueur
- ¼ oz. | 7.5 ml coconut syrup
- 2 dashes tiki bitters
- 2 drops 20% Saline Solution (see recipe on page 20)

1. Combine all of the ingredients in a cocktail shaker with ice and shake vigorously.
2. Strain the cocktail over fresh ice into a collins glass.
3. Garnish with a large mint sprig.

CARAWAY-INFUSED MEZCAL: In a jar, combine 2 tablespoons caraway seeds with 2 cups mezcal and allow the infusion to sit for 24 hours. Strain and bottle.

SPA WATER

This cucumber-and-kiwi cocktail is an homage to both the Hamptons—the inspiration behind The Montauk—and the multitude of spas across Arizona. Long known as a destination for health and wellness, some of the country's best spas are found in Phoenix, Scottsdale, Sedona, and beyond.

⫴

GLASSWARE: Collins glass
GARNISH: Dehydrated lime wheel

- 1½ oz. | 45 ml EFFEN Cucumber Vodka
- ¾ oz. | 22.5 ml Kiwi Reàl
- ½ oz. | 15 ml Barrow's Intense Ginger Liqueur
- 1 oz. | 30 ml club soda, to top

1. Combine all of the ingredients, except for the club soda, in a cocktail shaker with ice and shake.
2. Strain the cocktail into a collins glass with ice.
3. Top with the club soda and garnish with a dehydrated lime wheel.

ESPRESS YA' SELF

THE HOT CHICK
4363 NORTH 75TH STREET, SCOTTSDALE

Loud and boisterous with groovy vibes, The Hot Chick is a game bar full of nostalgia and late-night weekend partying. The numerous video, arcade, and board games provide entertainment in between sips from the playful drink menu. This cocktail twists the Espresso Martini with mezcal and cold brew; the caffeinated lift makes it the ideal drink to carry on the party all night long.

|||

GLASSWARE: Coupe glass

GARNISH: 3 to 4 coffee beans

- 1¼ oz. | 45 ml Absolut Vanilia Vodka
- 1 oz. | 30 ml fresh cold brew coffee
- ¾ oz. | 22.5 ml Grind Espresso Shot
- ½ oz. | 15 ml Rosaluna Mezcal Joven
- ½ oz. | 15 ml Simple Syrup (see recipe on page 20)

1. Combine all of the ingredients in a cocktail shaker with ice and shake thoroughly.
2. Strain the cocktail into a coupe and garnish 3 to 4 coffee beans.

ORANGE CARDAMOM ESPRESSO MARTINI

AMELIA'S BY EAT
8240 HAYDEN ROAD, B106, SCOTTSDALE

Amelia's by EAT is owned by chef Stacey Weber, who focuses on sourcing as many local ingredients as possible for her scratch-made menu. This includes local citrus for the orange cardamom syrup and partnering with Scottsdale-based vodka company ROXX. The cardamom brings a warmth to the espresso against the zing of the orange.

‖

GLASSWARE: Martini glass
GARNISH: Dehydrated orange slice

- 1½ oz. | 45 ml ROXX Vodka
- Double shot of espresso
- ½ oz. | 15 ml Orange Cardamom Syrup (see recipe)

1. Combine all of the ingredients in a cocktail shaker with ice and shake.
2. Strain the cocktail into a martini glass.
3. Garnish with a dehydrated orange slice.

ORANGE CARDAMOM SYRUP: Combine 1 cup water, 1 cup sugar, 4 sliced oranges, and 5 cardamom pods in a small pot and simmer on medium until the sugar dissolves. Don't change the heat level. Cool and store, but don't strain.

YOU'RE WELCOME

COURSE
7366 EAST SHEA BOULEVARD, SUITE 106,
SCOTTSDALE

COURSE manages to walk the fine line of being unpretentious while also proclaiming that this is no ordinary restaurant. Located in a strip mall, COURSE is both unfussy in approach while meticulous in presentation, something that carries into Nicholas Padua's cocktails like You're Welcome. The melon vodka and cucumber water make it refreshing while the absinthe spritz and pea bitters make it extraordinary.

GLASSWARE: Long-stemmed coupe glass
GARNISH: Pea tendril, 2 spritzes absinthe

- 2 oz. | 60 ml melon vodka
- 1 oz. | 30 ml Cucumber Water (see recipe on page 140)
- ½ oz. | 15 ml Simple Syrup (see recipe on page 20)
- ½ oz. | 15 ml fresh lime juice
- 5 dashes pea bitters

1. Place an ice sphere on an ice embellishment tray to stamp the ice.
2. Combine all of the ingredients in a cocktail shaker with ice and shake until properly diluted.
3. Remove the ice sphere from the tray and place with the textured side up it in a long-stemmed coupe.
4. Double-strain the cocktail over the ice cube.
5. To garnish, using bar tweezers, place the pea tendril on the ice sphere then spritz the drink's surface with the absinthe.

IT'S GOLD!

General manager Nicholas Padua and chef Cory Oppold have worked hard to make COURSE feel approachable, but sometimes you need to throw a little foie gras and gold on a drink to remind people they are in the presence of something special. This cocktail is fun and decadent and a reminder why dining out in Arizona can be such a great time.

GLASSWARE: Stemmed tulip spirit glass
GARNISH: One-eighth gold flake sheet, one-quarter demitasse foie gras powder

- 3 oz. | 90 ml Foie Gras Fat-Washed Rum (see recipe)
- 2 oz. | 60 ml sauternes
- ½ oz. | 15 ml Honey Syrup (see recipe on page 20)
- 1 oz. | 30 ml fresh lemon juice
- 4 dashes Bittermens 'Elemakule Tiki Bitters
- 4 dashes apple bitters
- 1 barspoon egg white powder

1. Combine all of the ingredients in a cocktail shaker with ice and shake vigorously for 30 seconds.
2. Double-strain the cocktail into a stemmed spirit glass.
3. Garnish using bar tweezers by placing the gold sheet over a quarter of the drink surface, starting at the rim, then sprinkle foie gras powder on the gold sheet.

FOIE GRAS FAT-WASHED RUM: In a saucepan over low heat, add 2 oz. foie gras and heat it until it becomes liquid. Add the rendered fat to 1 (750 ml) bottle of Ron Zacapa XO Rum in a large jar. Place the jar in the freezer overnight so that the fat congeals at the top of the mixture. Skim off the fat, then strain the rum through a chinois and rebottle.

CHARTREUPHY

COURSE

7366 EAST SHEA BOULEVARD, SUITE 106,
SCOTTSDALE

W hen ordered at the restaurant, the Chartreuphy cocktail is finished in a Nick & Nora glass but not before being distilled through a medicine bottle tableside first. Not every cocktail at COURSE comes with a theatrical presentation, but when one does, it's for the right reasons.

GLASSWARE: Nick & Nora glass

- 1 oz. | 30 ml Basil Hayden Bourbon
- ¾ oz. | 22.5 ml Green Chartreuse
- ¾ oz. | 22.5 ml Carpano Antica Formula Vermouth
- ½ oz. | 15 ml Del Maguey Vida Clásico
- ¼ oz. | 7.5 ml Campari
- ¼ oz. | 7.5 ml Aperol
- 2 dashes Bittermens 'Elemakule Tiki Bitters
- Orange peel, to express

1. Combine all of the ingredients, except for the orange peel, in a mixing glass.
2. Add ice and stir in continuous motion for 10 to 15 seconds or until properly diluted.
3. Express the orange peel over the drink and discard it.
4. Strain the cocktail into a Nick & Nora.

TIME STANDS STILL SAGE'ARITA

LINCOLN STEAKHOUSE & BAR
5402 EAST LINCOLN DRIVE, SCOTTSDALE

This savory twist on a Margarita comes from Ricky Cutten at JW Marriott's Scottsdale Camelback Inn Resort & Spa. The cocktail's name is borrowed from the resort's motto—"Where Time Stands Still"—that is proudly displayed on the clock tower. Served at the signature Lincoln Steakhouse & Bar, the recipe calls for a sage agave syrup, which the restaurant crafts with sage from their garden.

‖

GLASSWARE: Etched rocks glass
GARNISH: Dehydrated orange half-moon

- **Salt, for the rim**
- **1½ oz. | 45 ml Casamigos Reposado Tequila**
- **½ oz. | 15ml Sage Agave Syrup (see recipe)**
- **½ oz. | 15 ml fresh lime juice**
- **½ oz. | 15 ml grapefruit juice**
- **¼ oz. | 7.5 ml Cointreau**

1. Dip the rim of a rocks glass in water then dip the rim in salt. Combine the remaining ingredients in a Boston shaker with ice and shake.

2. Strain the cocktail into the rimmed glass over fresh ice.

3. Garnish with a dehydrated orange wheel half.

SAGE AGAVE SYRUP: Combine 1 cup agave nectar with 1 cup hot water and stir to combine. Add 1 bunch fresh sage leaves and stir. Allow the syrup to steep, then strain and store it in the refrigerator.

EL CADILLAC

This deconstructed Cadillac Margarita makes the drink a more immersive and interactive experience. "People often ask me how to drink this," says Abby Kate Larson, corporate mixologist for The Maggiore Group. "The answer is, however you want—there's no wrong way! Personally, I would pour half of that sidecar over the top of the margarita, shoot the rest of the sidecar, bite that cinnamon orange, and then take my time sipping the big one, because you look really cool doing it."

GLASSWARE: Snifter, shot glass, mini-snifter

GARNISH: Edible gold flakes, cinnamon-grated orange wheel, salt, lime wheel, flaming cinnamon stick

---

- 1½ oz. | 45 ml Patrón Silver tequila
- ¾ oz. | 22.5 ml agave syrup (1:1 ratio of agave to water)
- 1½ oz. | 45 ml fresh lime juice
- ½ oz. | 15 ml Cointreau
- 1 oz. | 30 ml Grand Marnier Cordon Rouge, for the sidecar

1. Wet the rim of a snifter then dip the rim in salt. Combine all of the ingredients, except for the Grand Marnier, in a cocktail shaker with ice and shake vigorously.

2. Strain the cocktail over fresh ice into the salt-rimmed snifter.

3. Garnish with edible gold flakes and the lime wheel.

4. Next, pour the Grand Marnier into a mini-snifter for the sidecar.

5. Take a cinnamon stick and grate it over a freshly sliced orange wheel, covering the fruit. Place the orange and the cinnamon stick into the shot glass.

6. Ignite the cinnamon with a hand torch, charring until the it is fragrant and smoking.

7. Use your favorite gold tray and place all three items on top to serve.

THE JALISCO OLD FASHIONED

THE MEXICANO
4801 EAST CACTUS ROAD, SCOTTSDALE

This take on an Old Fashioned substitutes the whiskey for a reposado, a "relaxed" expression of tequila that brings in a taste reminiscent of whiskey. This recipe uses Alma Tepec, which is a Oaxacan chile liqueur made with rare, ancestral pasilla chiles. It also uses an oleo saccharum, which is a syrup that is made with fruit or peels and sugar. It's a great way to use up scraps while creating a fun ingredient for cocktails.

GLASSWARE: Double rocks glass

GARNISH: Pineapple slice, charred; Luxardo maraschino cherry

- 1½ oz. | 45 ml JAJA Reposado Tequila
- ½ oz. | 15 ml Alma Tepec Licor de Chile Pasilla Mixe
- 2 dashes Angostura bitters
- ½ oz. | 15 ml Pineapple Oleosaccharum (see recipe)
- 2 dashes Bittermens Xocolatl Mole Bitters

1. Build all of the ingredients, in the order listed, in a glass mixing vessel and add ice.
2. Stir the drink for 40 rotations.
3. Using a julep strainer, strain the cocktail over a large ice cube.
4. Garnish with a thin slice of pineapple that has been charred on both sides with a hand torch, skewered with a Luxardo maraschino cherry.

PINEAPPLE OLEOSACCHARUM: To make, put a 1:1 ratio of sugar and the fruit or peel in a sealed glass jar and let sit for 24 at room temperature before straining.

THE VALLEY

CINCO DE MAYO

COPPER COSMO MARTINI

PINEAPPLE COCONUT MOJITO

HIBISCUS MARGARITA

COTTON

CITRUS

CLIMATE

MARG AL MELONE

TRÉ CUCUMBER

THE PICK ME UP

DEVIL GIN FIZZ

I know it doesn't quite seem right to pack the remainder of metro Phoenix into one chapter when it covers so many miles and so many great cities that make up the rest of the Valley. But in the same vein, so many places around the rest of the state are worth the drive as well—we are spoiled for choice here!

This book has focused a lot on Phoenix and Scottsdale, and as you read, there's a good reason for that. However, the future is looking so bright for the East and West Valleys in places like Queen Creek, Gilbert, Goodyear, Litchfield Park, and Buckeye, and I expect we'll see the names of award winners coming out of these cities before very long. They're already off to a good start, as you'll see in the pages that follow.

CUCUMBER THYME SIMPLE SYRUP: Make Simple Syrup (see recipe on page 20), adding a sprig of fresh thyme and cucumber slices, to taste, to the sauce-pan as the syrup cooks. Muddle, allow the syrup to cool, then double strain.

CINCO DE MAYO

ESPIRITU MESA
123 WEST MAIN STREET, MESA

There is a historical context to this mezcal-and-sparkling wine combo by bartender Adrian Galindo. "Commemorating the Battle of Puebla and the victory of Mexican forces over the French, this cocktail takes a classic French 75 build and revamps it with a combination of French and Mexican ingredients," he says. "Viva la Revolución."

‖

GLASSWARE: Fluted glass

GARNISH: Rosemary, cucumber slice

- 1½ oz. | 45 ml mezcal
- ¾ oz. | 22.5 ml elderflower liqueur
- ¾ oz. | 22.5 ml fresh lemon juice
- ¾ oz. | 22.5 ml Cucumber Thyme Simple Syrup (see recipe)
- 2 oz. | 60 ml sparkling white French wine, to top

1. Combine all of the ingredients, except for the wine, in a cocktail shaker with ice and shake until cold.

2. Double-strain the cocktail into a fluted glass and top with the wine.

3. Garnish with a sprig of fresh rosemary and a cucumber slice.

COPPER COSMO MARTINI

LITCHFIELD'S
300 EAST WIGWAM BOULEVARD, LITCHFIELD PARK

L itchfield's is the signature dining and drinking establishment at the historic Wigwam Resort. Located in the West Valley, the resort is tucked back in the charming downtown district of Litchfield Park. Litchfield's draws on the area's agricultural heritage and Old West traditions for its menu, with vibrant and citrusy cocktails that pair well with its fire-forward offerings.

GLASSWARE: Copper coupe glass

GARNISH: Flower

- 2 oz. | 60 ml Absolut Elyx Vodka
- 1 oz. | 30 ml Cointreau
- ½ oz. | 7 ml fresh lime juice
- ½ oz. | 7 ml cranberry juice
- Splash Simple Syrup (see recipe on page 20)

1. Combine all of the ingredients in a cocktail shaker with ice and shake until well mixed.
2. Pour the cocktail into a coupe and garnish with a flower.

PINEAPPLE COCONUT MOJITO

LITCHFIELD'S
300 EAST WIGWAM BOULEVARD, LITCHFIELD PARK

The Pineapple Coconut Mojito embraces the essence of the tropics, which, while out of place in the desert, is a good fit for the lush landscape of the Wigwam Resort. Somewhat off the beaten path of metro Phoenix, the property is bursting with flowers and palm trees, which makes sipping one of these light and refreshing cocktails a perfect combination.

GLASSWARE: Highball glass
GARNISH: Mint, pineapple leaves

- 1½ oz. | 45 ml Kula Toasted Coconut Rum
- 1 oz. | 30 ml pineapple juice
- ½ oz. | 15 ml fresh lime juice
- 5 mint leaves

1. Combine all of the ingredients in a cocktail shaker with ice and shake until well mixed.
2. Pour the cocktail over ice into a highball.
3. Garnish with additional mint and pineapple leaves.

HIBISCUS MARGARITA

LITCHFIELD'S
300 EAST WIGWAM BOULEVARD, LITCHFIELD PARK

This cocktail takes inspiration from the hibiscus blooms that brighten The Wigwam's surrounding Sonoran landscape," says Audrey O'Kelly, Litchfield's general manager. "It embodies the spirit of Arizona." The team makes their own hibiscus syrup in-house, but it is possible to find it premade from brands like Monin and Torani.

|||

GLASSWARE: Margarita glass
GARNISH: Lime wheel, dried hibiscus flower

- Salt, for the rim
- 1½ oz. | 44 ml Don Julio Blanco Tequila
- ½ oz. | 15 ml fresh lime juice
- ½ oz. | 15 ml hibiscus syrup
- ½ oz. | 15 ml agave nectar

1. Wet the rim of a margarita glass then dip the rim in salt. Combine the remaining ingredients in a cocktail shaker with ice and shake enthusiastically until mixed.
2. Fill the rimmed margarita glass with fresh ice.
3. Strain the shaker into the glass and garnish with a lime wheel and a dried hibiscus flower.

JOSHUA JAMES, CLEVER KOI AND FELLOW OSTERIA & PIZZERIA

What is your favorite cocktail to make?

The Old Fashioned.

How did you get interested in cocktails and mixology?

It started with my appreciation for history because most of the spirits we use date back centuries. And even the cocktails, while more recent, are all timepieces that teach you about a particular moment in history. I really love really digging into that.

What influences you as a mixologist?

At this point in my career, it's about mentoring the people we work with, showing them how to mix the creative aspects of the job with the need to serve everything in a timely manner. It's also about how to make mixology make sense from a business perspective, and how to really build a menu. That's my creative outlet now—helping grow the knowledge of our team and letting them express their creativity to make our menus better.

What do you find unique about Arizona's cocktail culture?

It's such a robust scene compared to ten years ago, which also means it's easier to keep talented young bartenders here in the state, instead of them leaving for bigger opportunities. That change has definitely buoyed the local bartending scene and has reached the point where it's self-sustaining, raising both the standards and also the talent level.

What are some underrated ingredients you love to use and why?

One thing we always do on our menu is offer two or three really good stirred or mixed cocktails with a low ABV. It's just a great option to have, so I'd say session cocktails are our secret ingredient.

What's one thing about Arizona that you think people don't understand or is misconstrued?

For people who haven't been here in a while, they often think it's a corporate food wasteland, and truth be told, it was that for a long time. But now, from downtown Phoenix to all these little neighborhood pockets all across the Valley and the state, there are these really great hotspots and hidden gems with so much personality versus the big-box new-build perception. There is a lot of history here, especially if you venture beyond the trendy nightlife scene.

What's an accomplishment or point of pride in your career?

Clever Koi in Phoenix just celebrated ten years, which is a trip. We're proud to look back and think of so many great people who have come and gone on to found their own places and make a mark—on top of all the amazing people working for us right now.

Do you have any final thoughts?

The most important thing in our industry is also often overlooked, and that's that it is a people business. You can have the best food and amazing drinks, but that's just the pathway to the guest and to launch a dialogue. I've loved working in bars, but what really sticks with you are the relationships and the people you interact with. And that can get lost in the social media age where everything is so image based, but when you go somewhere, it's the memories and connections that you'll always remember. We've always said we want our restaurant to be the sort of place we'd want to work because of the relationships with the people, and I'm proud that founding principal of our partnership still stands ten years later.

COTTON

TWENTY6
5350 EAST MARRIOTT DRIVE, PHOENIX

Copper, Cattle, Citrus, Cotton, and Climate—these are the 5 Cs of Arizona. Near the turn of the twentieth century, cotton became king of the crops in Arizona. The profitability was due in part of the new Pima long-staple cotton. Today, the state remains one of the leaders in cotton production. This pleasantly simple cocktail from Twenty6 pays homage to that history with a sweet twist.

GLASSWARE: Martini glass
GARNISH: Cotton candy

- **2 oz. | 60 ml Grey Goose Vodka**
- **½ oz. | 15 ml fresh lemon juice**
- **½ oz. | 15 ml Simple Syrup (see recipe on page 20)**

1. Combine all of the ingredients in a cocktail shaker with ice and shake vigorously.
2. Strain the cocktail into a martini glass.
3. Garnish with a fluffy pile of cotton candy.

CITRUS

Arizona thrives at citrus production; it's not uncommon for residents to have grapefruit, lemon, or lime trees in their yards. Citrus farming was made possible in the mid-1800s due to the work put into irrigation systems, including canals from the Hohokam culture that were rediscovered and are still in use today.

GLASSWARE: Martini glass

GARNISH: Lemon twist

- 2 oz. | 60 ml Absolut Grapefruit Vodka
- 1 oz. | 30 ml fresh grapefruit juice
- 2 dashes Peychaud's bitters

1. Combine all of the ingredients in a cocktail shaker with ice and shake.
2. Strain the cocktail into a martini glass.
3. Delicately garnish with a lemon twist.

CLIMATE

TWENTY6
5350 EAST MARRIOTT DRIVE, PHOENIX

The 5 Cs of Arizona played an important role in the agricultural economy during the state's early history. Today, they are more culturally relevant than economically impactful. Enjoy this salute to one of those 5 Cs.

GLASSWARE: Martini glass
GARNISH: Luxardo maraschino cherries

- **2 oz. | 60 ml Aviation American Gin**
- **¾ oz. | 22.5 ml fresh lemon juice**
- **½ oz. | 15 ml maraschino liqueur**
- **¼ oz. | 7.5 ml crème de violette**

1. Combine all of the ingredients in a cocktail shaker with ice and, with enthusiasm, shake everything up.
2. Strain the cocktail into a martini glass.
3. Garnish with maraschino cherries.

MARG AL MELONE

This cocktail was meant to complement and invoke the spirit of the refreshing Italian summer dish *prosciutto e melone*, with light, airy cantaloupe foam and crisp mint. It is aromatic, crushable, and with perfect body. "I originally made this cocktail for a cocktail competition honoring International Women's Month," says Abby Kate Larson. "It found a home on The Sicilian Butcher's menu, where people can enjoy the drink across the Valley on a warm summer day."

GLASSWARE: Coupe glass
GARNISH: Cantaloupe melon ball, mint sprig

- 1½ oz. | 45 ml Tres Generaciones Tequila Plata
- 1 oz. | 30 ml fresh lime juice
- ¾ oz. | 22.5 ml Melonade Aperitif
- ¾ oz. | 22.5 ml Honey Syrup (see recipe on page 20)
- 5 mint leaves
- Cantaloupe Foam (see recipe), to top

1. Combine all of the ingredients, except for the foam, in a cocktail shaker with ice and shake vigorously.
2. Double-strain the cocktail into a coupe.
3. Use a whipping siphon to top with Cantaloupe Foam.
4. Garnish with a mint sprig and a melon ball.

CANTALOUPE FOAM: Combine 10 oz. (300 ml) egg whites, 5 oz. (150 ml) Melonade Aperitif, 4 oz. (120 ml) fresh lime juice, and 4 oz. (120 ml) Simple Syrup (see recipe on page 20) in a mixing vessel, then carefully pour the mixture into a whipping siphon. Seal the siphon well and attach a cartridge. Always keep the foam chilled and shake vigorously before dispensing.

TRÉ CUCUMBER

POSTINO WINECAFE
VARIOUS LOCATIONS

Postino has been a mainstay of the Phoenix happy hour scene since the early 2000s. Co-founders Craig and Kris DeMarco were inspired while traveling around Italy and watching residents build personal connections over snacks and lunches. They came up with the idea of shared bruschetta boards and opened the first Postino Wine-Cafe in the historic Arcadia Post Office. Since then, locations have cropped up all around the state and even in nearby states. A newly introduced cocktail menu has bolstered the offerings, like this light and lovely cucumber-inspired drink.

‖

GLASSWARE: Coupe glass

GARNISH: Cucumber slice

- 1 oz. | 30 ml vodka
- ¾ oz. | 22.5 ml Caravella Limoncello
- ½ oz. | 15 ml Honey Syrup (see recipe on page 20)
- ½ oz. | 15 ml fresh lemon juice
- ½ oz. | 15 ml fresh cucumber juice

1. Chill a coupe glass. Combine all of the ingredients in a cocktail shaker with ice and shake.
2. Strain the cocktail into the chilled coupe.
3. Garnish with a cucumber slice resting on the rim of the glass.

THE PICK ME UP

BRODY'S ITALIAN
10810 NORTH TATUM BOULEVARD, SUITE #107,
PHOENIX

Sometimes all you need is a classic to round out the night, and Jason Brody's Espresso Martini, served at his Brody's Italian restaurant, fits the bill. Even better, the recipe uses Scottsdale-based ROXX Vodka.

GLASSWARE: Martini glass

GARNISH: 3 coffee beans

- 1½ oz. | 45 ml ROXX Vodka
- ½ oz. | 15 ml white crème de cacao
- 1 oz. | 30 ml Kahlúa
- 1½ oz. | 45 ml Caffé D'arte Espresso

1. Combine all of the ingredients in a cocktail shaker and shake until there's foam in the shaker.
2. Strain the cocktail into a martini glass.
3. Garnish with 3 coffee beans.

DEVIL GIN FIZZ

PEDAL HAUS BREWERY
730 SOUTH MILL AVENUE #102, TEMPE

I n 2015, Pedal Haus Brewery was started as a way for founder Julian Wright to combine his love of cycling with local craft brews. The microbrewery has been a success, with bike-themed decor and award-winning brews, growing to multiple locations and expanding offerings beyond beer. The Devil Gin Fizz incorporates one of their newest products, a hard seltzer, with passion fruit puree—a perfect way to kick things off for a night out in Tempe. If you can't get your hands on this particular seltzer, use a blackberry hard seltzer of your choice.

GLASSWARE: Munique glass
GARNISH: Mint sprig

- 1½ oz. | 45 ml Hendrick's Gin
- 1 oz. | 30 ml passion fruit puree
- ½ oz. |15 ml fresh lemon juice
- 5 mint leaves
- Pedal Haus Brewery Adult Soda Pop Hard Seltzer, to top

1. Combine all of the ingredients, except for the seltzer, in a cocktail shaker with ice and shake.
2. Fill a munique glass with ice.
3. Strain the cocktail into the glass.
4. Top with blackberry seltzer and garnish with a sprig of mint.

PHOTO CREDITS

Pages 31, 32, 35, 36 Rachelle Connolly; page 55 suspence.com; page 68 Kyle Arthur; pages 86–87, 89, 91, 93, 184 Grace Stufkosky; page 95 Wendy Rose Gould; page 97 Josue Orozco; pages 99, 101 Shelby Moore; pages 119, 120, 123, 124 Nader Abushhab; pages 126, 129, 130 Ryan Cordwell; pages 133, 135, 136 Sterling Godwin Photography; pages 139, 141, 256–257 Born & Raised Hospitality; pages 150, 153, 154 Wyatt Rutt Photography; page 161 Justin Yee; pages 162, 165, 166, 168, 246 Kayla McKernan; page 171 Jessica Honea; page 174 Ashley Guice Creative; page 177 Alec Gonzalez; page 179 Ashley Cibor; pages 191, 192, 239, 241 Jill McNamara; pages 195, 197 Autumn Harmony West; pages 203, 204, 207, 209, 211 Fairmont Scottsdale Princess; pages 224, 227 Jocque Concepts; page 228 ROXX Vodka; page 265 Nadya Sanchez; page 269 Joanie Simon; page 270 Bailey Mosley.

Pages 1, 3, 4–5, 6, 8 (top), 10, 11, 14, 16, 22–23, 56–57, 82–83, 156–157, 186–187, 242–243, 276–277 used under official license from Shutterstock.com.

Pages 7, 8 (bottom), 9, 12, 13, courtesy of the Library of Congress.

All other images courtesy of the respective bars, restaurants, and interviewees.

ACKNOWLEDGMENTS

What an enormous pleasure it was putting *Arizona Cocktails* together; many thanks to the team at Cider Mill Press and HarperCollins Focus for approaching me to write this book. It's been an honor.

To every bartender, bar owner, PR representative, and anyone else I have collaborated with while putting together this book, thank you for your time and your patience. We got there in the end, and I am so proud of the result!

My thanks to God for this and every other opportunity I have been blessed with.

Mom—thanks for being a lifelong and willing copywriter and editor. It's finally paid off.

Dad—thank you for always being a champion and supporter of everything I do.

Andrea—you are always a phone call or text away whenever I need that extra ear or support. I don't know how you do it, but I'm so glad you do. Our friendship is invaluable to me.

Justin—what would I do without you? Knowing I can count on you for anything, from the mundane to the serious, is priceless. I appreciate your constant enthusiasm to participate in cocktail tasting.

And finally, to Willie D—I can only pursue this path because you ensure that the road is clear for me to get there. I can't be who I am without you, nor would I want to be. Idly.

ABOUT THE AUTHOR

Born in Colorado and raised in Arizona, author Asonta Benetti has spent her entire life in the West. A freelance writer, she specializes in beverage, food, and travel. Her work on spirits includes *Food & Wine*, VinePair, and InsideHook; other credits include Thrillist, *Bon Appétit*, AFAR, and *Phoenix New Times*, among others. She currently lives in Phoenix.

CONVERSION CHART

	1 dash		0.625 ml
	4 dashes		2.5 ml
	1 teaspoon		5 ml
¼ oz.			7.5 ml
⅓ oz.	2 teaspoons		10 ml
½ oz.	3 teaspoons	1 tablespoon	15 ml
⅔ oz.	4 teaspoons		20 ml
¾ oz.			22.5 ml
17/20 oz.			25 ml
1 oz.		2 tablespoons	30 ml
1½ oz.		3 tablespoons	45 ml
1¾ oz.			52.5 ml
2 oz.	4 tablespoons	¼ cup	60 ml
8 oz.		1 cup	250 ml
16 oz.	1 pint	2 cups	500 ml
24 oz.		3 cups	750 ml
32 oz.	1 quart	4 cups	1 liter (1,000 ml)

INDEX

—ABOUT CIDER MILL PRESS BOOK PUBLISHERS—

Good ideas ripen with time. From seed to harvest, Cider Mill Press brings fine reading, information, and entertainment together between the covers of its creatively crafted books. Our Cider Mill bears fruit twice a year, publishing a new crop of titles each spring and fall.

"Where Good Books Are Ready for Press"
501 Nelson Place
Nashville, Tennessee 37214
cidermillpress.com

RAILROAD AND COUNTY MAP OF

ARIZONA.

Geo. F. Cram, Engraver and Publisher, Chicago.

EXPLANATION

Railroads	Undsisted R.R.	Money Order P.O.
STATE CAPITOL	County Seat	

WELLS FARGO & CO.
OPERATE ALL ROADS.